MVFOL

Came to believe...

The spiritual adventure of A.A. as experienced
by individual members

Alcoholics Anonymous® World Services, Inc., New York

The following material is copyrighted © by The A.A. Grapevine, Inc. (excerpted from articles in the issues noted), and is reprinted with permission: "From Loneliness to Solitude" (September 1967), "Happiness" (April 1965), "Getting Ahead" (October 1964), "Ecstasy" (October 1965), "No Man Is an Island" (July 1967). "Reason or Conscience?" is reprinted from *The Tom-Tom* (July 1956).

Came to Believe . . .
Copyright © 1973 by
Alcoholics Anonymous World Services, Inc.
475 Riverside Drive, New York, NY 10115
Mail address:
Box 459, Grand Central Station, New York, NY 10163
All rights reserved under Pan-American copyright convention
International copyright reserved

Twenty-second printing 1995

*This is A.A. General Service
Conference-approved literature*

ALCOHOLICS ANONYMOUS and A.A. are registered trademarks ® of A.A. World Services, Inc.

Library of Congress Catalog Card No. 73-164457
ISBN 0-916856-05-4
Printed in the United States of America
Alcoholics Anonymous ®

75M—10/95

CONTENTS

FOREWORD

Five years of preparation and earnest thought have gone into this booklet, since an A.A. member first pointed out the need for it. The description of Alcoholics Anonymous as "a spiritual program" has been confusing to some newcomers, many of whom tend to translate "spiritual" as "religious." But, as our co-founder Doctor Bob said (in an A.A. Grapevine article), "We are not bound by theological doctrine. . . . We are many minds in our organization."

"Came to Believe . . ." is designed as an outlet for the rich diversity of convictions implied in "God *as we understood Him*." Most of the material was written expressly for the booklet, in response to an appeal issued by the General Service Office. The places of origin shown for each story or brief comment indicate how widespread this response was. And the Fellowship can be grateful to *all* those who took the trouble to set down their spiritual journeys in writing, whether or not their contributions appear in this booklet. Without such a broad view of membership thinking, it would not have been possible to make a truly representative selection.

Originally, our co-founder Bill W. planned to write a foreword. In lieu of this, the introductions to each section reflect Bill's outlook, already on record in the book "As Bill Sees It."

1

"SPIRITUAL"?

> *Do not let
> any prejudice you may
> have against spiritual
> terms deter you from
> honestly asking yourself
> what they might mean
> to you.*

> *Bill W.*

THE OPENING TO THE SPIRITUAL WORLD

A.A. is a spiritual program and a spiritual way of life. Even the first half of the First Step, "We admitted we were powerless over alcohol," is a spiritual experience. An A.A. member needs more than physical capabilities; he needs the use of his full faculties as a human being to hear the message, to think about it, to review the effects of the past, to realize, to admit, and to accept. These processes are activities of the mind, which is part of the spirit.

Yes, I began with blind faith, but the proof of truth is that *it works.* I believed those who said they had suffered from alcoholism, but, through A.A., were now enjoying sobriety. So the truth was there for me to see. But shortly I knew the truth from my own experience. I was not only released from the compulsion to drink; I was guided toward a compulsion to live!

A.A. also made me very much aware, by constant repetition, of my freedom of choice, and this is the human faculty of willpower. As time has gone on in sobriety, I have been offered and have used the opportunity to learn more about humanity by learning more about myself. I now realize that when I first said at an A.A. meeting, "My name is Tom and I am an alcoholic," I was expressing the first truth I had known about myself. Think of the spirituality in such statements. My name tells me that I am a human being; the fact that I *can* know it, think about it, and communicate it reinforces my humanity and makes me aware and excited that I *am!*

This, then, became the opening to the spiritual world. With the guidance of the program and the encouragement and examples within the Fellowship, I could begin to find out about myself and be prepared to accept what I found. I learned in the Fellowship that if others could accept me and love me as I was, then I should love myself as I was—not for what I was, but for what I could become. So I have learned a little about my mind and about my will and about my emotions and passions.

I have learned that I can be a good human being, although an imperfect one; that, when I consciously live in the real world (sanity), each good day helps to counterbalance my past.

My religion did not give me A.A. A.A. gave me greater strength in my religion. The simple contrast between active alcoholism and active sobriety has helped me to seek, to listen, and to apply the good principles of living, and I am rewarded with much more excitement and joy than was mine before A.A. sobriety. By accepting this sobriety gratefully, as a gift, and using it willingly, I have become aware of other gifts available to me as a human being. To get the benefits, I need only ask and then use.

This is the crux of the program and the crux of living: acceptance and action.

The gift of understanding has allowed the simple messages from my parents, my teachers, and my church to take on new meaning and soundness. With the gift of serenity, I am ready and willing to accept what God permits to happen to me; with the gift of courage, to take action to change the things I can for the good of myself and others. The gift of wisdom has been given to me so that in personal relationships I may act intelligently and with love or, as it has also been expressed, with competence and compassion.

Now I am trying to grasp the idea of living "inside out." The Big Book, "As Bill Sees It—the A.A. Way of Life," "24 Hours a Day," the meetings, the experiences, the consciousness of change in myself, in my thinking, my choices, and my habits—all of these are spiritual. There is the spirituality of the A.A. way of life, which simply makes us aware of our individual inner resources. There is no materialism in A.A.—just spirituality. If we take care of our inner needs, our other needs will be provided for.

I have come to believe that the gift of sobriety is what gives value and dignity to my life. It is this that I have to share, and it grows as it is shared.

El Cerrito, California

HOW FORTUNATE WE ARE

I call Kinlochard my spiritual home. It is a wee hamlet nestling in a valley between the hills and on the banks of Loch Ard. I never tire of gazing across it to the forest on the far side, with its hundreds of shades of green, reflected in the surface of the loch. Peregrine falcons are nesting on the crags above, and the heron slowly wings its way up the loch to its nest in the huge trees on a small island. The swans, mallard, and grayback ducks share the banks with sandpipers and coots and a few fishermen, casting for trout. Sometimes I can see, far up the hill, a stag and a hind crossing a clearing and, if I am lucky, a couple of otters playing on the rocks beside the loch. Peace prevails.

When I first discovered Kinlochard, I was on one of my prolonged binges. Even then, the beauty and tranquillity got through the alcoholic haze. Now that I have sobriety, I try to visit this place of rest twice a year and marvel at the majesty of our Creator. I see no beauty in art. Sculpture and architecture are man-made and cannot rival the Creator's work. How can we hope to better the Master who taught us? How fortunate we alcoholics are to have a malady which compels us to seek recovery through the spiritual.

Egremont, England

A.A. IS A PHILOSOPHY

A religion, properly, is of divine origin; governs the person in his relationship with his Higher Power; and promises its rewards and punishments after death. A philosophy is of human origin; governs the person in his relationship with his fellowman; and promises its rewards and punishments during life. A.A., I submit, is a philosophy. If we alcoholics follow the philosophy of A.A., we can regain an understanding of our several religions.

Maryland

IN HIS OWN INDIVIDUAL RIGHT

Spirituality is an awakening—or is it all the loose ends woven together into a mellow fabric? It's understanding—or is it all the knowledge one need ever know? It's freedom—if you consider fear slavery. It's confidence—or is it the belief that a higher power will see you through any storm or gale? It's adhering to the dictates of your conscience—or is it a deep, genuine, living concern for the people and the planet? It's peace of mind in the face of adversity. It's a keen and sharpened desire for survival.

It's a man or a woman. It's gratitude for every happenstance of the past that brought you to a moment of justice. It's the joy of being a young man in a young world. It's awareness—or is it realization of one's capabilities and limitations? It's concentration—or is it an easy sensing of the universe? It's seeing a mystical power for good in each and every human being. It's patience in the face of stupidity. It's feeling that you want to knock somebody's head off—and walking away instead. It's when you're down past your last dime, and you know you still have something that money can't buy. It's wearing dungarees that feel like a tuxedo. It's wanting to go home, yet being there. It's a rocket ride that goes far beyond the world your eye can see. It's looking at something that superficially is ugly, but radiates beauty. It's a majestic skyline or a western desert. It's a young child. It's seeing a caterpillar turn into a butterfly. It's the awareness that survival is a savage fight between you and yourself. It's a magnetic pull toward those who are down and out. It's knowing that even the bad times are good.

Don't look back—you haven't seen anything yet.

When people look at you and wonder what's with you, the look in your eyes will answer them: "Because I can cut it!"

The singular thing that is spirituality cannot be given to a fellowman by word of mouth. If every man is to have it, then every man must earn it, in his own way, by his own hand, stamped by the seal of himself, in his own individual right.

New York, New York

THE OTHER SIDE

During a meeting one day, I remarked that I was just tickled to death with this A.A. program—all but the spiritual side of it.

After the meeting, another member came up to me and said, "I liked that remark you made—about how you like the program—all but the spiritual part of it. We've got a little time. Why don't we talk about the *other* side of it?"

That ended the conversation.

Modesto, California

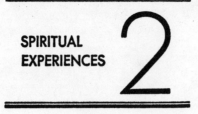

SPIRITUAL EXPERIENCES

2

*It is certain that all recipients
of spiritual experiences
declare for their reality.
The best evidence of that reality
is in the subsequent fruits.
Those who receive these gifts
of grace are very much
changed people, almost invariably
for the better.*

Bill W.

Talk, 1960

HE HAD BEEN LISTENING

In my early youth, I was confronted with a choice: what seemed to be a dull, moral life or what appeared to be an exciting, adventurous life— after a few drinks of alcohol. I had been brought up in the tradition of a stern and vengeful God, who was watching every move I made. I could not work up too much love for that type of deity, and I felt guilty about it. But after a drink or two, I would forget my guilt. This, I decided, was the life for me!

It started off pleasantly enough, promoting dreams of glittering fame and fortune. But this life gradually regressed to a constant night-mare of fear and remorse over my condition and resentment and anger at a normal way of life which went on all around me, but which appar-ently I could not enter. The truth was that I drank myself out of society, coming by degrees to live in a mental state that sealed off any social or moral contact with anybody. But at that time I could not see my ex-cessive drinking as the cause. I had become convinced that God and society had frozen me out, denying me the breaks in life. I could see no sense in living. I lacked the courage to kill myself, but I believe that desperation would have broken this barrier of cowardice had it not been for an experience that changed my mental outlook entirely.

This experience came about through the death of my father in Scotland. He had lived a good life in his community and was honored in his passing by all who had known him. I had received newspapers giving accounts of his funeral. That evening, I was seated at a small table in a crowded tavern, drunk and brooding over what I had read. I felt no sorrow at my father's passing. Hate and envy saturated my mind, and I was muttering to myself, "Why should he and other people get all the breaks in life, while good men like me don't get a chance? What a rotten deal I'm getting! People would love and honor me, too, if I had the chances in life he had."

In the tavern, the noise of conversation was deafening. But suddenly I heard a voice in my mind ring out loud and clear: "What accounting are you going to give to God of your life?" I looked around, astounded, for it was my grandmother's voice. She had passed from this life and out of my thoughts over twenty years earlier. This was her favorite quotation. I had heard her say it often in my youth, and now I heard it again in the tavern.

As soon as I heard this voice, my mind cleared up, and I knew beyond all doubt that no other person nor any situation was responsible for my state. I alone was responsible.

The effect was shattering. First, I had heard that voice, and then my whole excuse for my failure in life—that I had never got any breaks —was wiped out of my mind forever. The thought hit me that if I killed myself, as I wanted to, there was a chance that I might meet up with God, and have to give Him an account of the life I lived, with no one else to blame for it. I wanted no part of that, and the idea of killing myself was dropped then and there. But the thought that I might die at any time remained to haunt me.

All this was crazy, I thought. But, no matter how much I argued with myself that I was having a hallucination, I could not dismiss the implication of the experience. I could visualize myself being brought before a stern-looking deity, who would coldly look down His nose at me with utter contempt and say grimly, "Speak up!" That was as far as my imagination would carry me, and from then on I would get blind drunk trying to blot out the whole experience. But when I came to in the morning, the experience would still be with me, strong as ever.

I thought I had better quit drinking for a while and start to reshape my life. This resolution led to a terrible shock. Up to this time, I had never tied in my troubles with alcohol. I knew that I drank too much, but I had always felt that I had good reason to drink. Now I found, to my amazement and horror, that I could not quit. Drinking had become such a part of my life that I could not function without it.

I did not know where to turn for help. Believing that people thought about me the way I thought about them, I was sure I could not turn to them. This left only God, and if He felt about me as I felt about Him, this was a slim hope indeed. In this manner, I passed through the three blackest months of my life. During that time, it seemed, I drank more than I ever had before, and I prayed to "nothing" for help to get away from alcohol.

One morning, I came to on the floor in my room, horribly sick, convinced that God was not going to listen to me. More on reflex than anything else, I got to work that morning and attempted to make up a payroll, though it was hard to hold my shaking hands still enough to put the figures in the right place. After a great deal of trouble, I finally completed the job. With a sigh of relief, I looked out the window and noticed a man approaching the hut I was working in. As I recognized him, hate surged into my mind. Seven months before, he had had the temerity to ask me in front of other men if I was having trouble with my drinking, and I had been deeply insulted by his question. I had not seen him for months, but my hatred of him was alive and vital as he passed by the hut.

Then something happened that has never ceased to amaze me. As he moved out of sight, everything went blank. The next thing I knew, I was standing before him outside the hut, hearing myself ask him whether he would help me to stop drinking. If I had consciously decided to ask any individual for help, he would have been the last man I would have approached! He smiled and said that he would try to help me, and he brought me to the A.A. recovery program.

In thinking all this over, it finally became obvious to me that the God I thought had judged and damned me had done nothing of the sort. He had been listening, and in His own good time His answer came. His answer was threefold: the opportunity for a life of sobriety; Twelve Steps to practice, in order to attain and maintain that life of sobriety; fellowship within the program, ever ready to sustain and help me each twenty-four-hour day.

I hold no illusion that *I* brought the A.A. program of recovery into my life. I must always consider it as a gift of opportunity. In the use of this opportunity, the onus is on me.

St. John's, Newfoundland

A PRESENCE

I am a radio officer on a tanker, and the final revelation of my condition and its cure came while I was sitting alone in my stateroom with my favorite bottle. I asked for God's help out loud, although only my own ears could hear. Suddenly, there was a Presence in the room, bringing a peculiar warmth, a changed, softer shade of light, and an immense feeling of relief. Though I was sober enough, I said to myself, "You're drunk again," and I went to bed.

In the morning, however—in broad daylight—the Presence was still there. I was not hung-over, either. I realized that I had asked and I had received. From that time on, I have had no alcohol. Whenever I get the urge, I think of that which happened to me, and it keeps me straight.

A.A. Internationalists

FRESH SNOW

Exposed to the Fellowship of A.A. for over six years, I had known in that time three relapses, brutal and dismal episodes. Each increased my self-abasement and hopelessness. Sober once again, settled into a minor job, I learned that there was satisfaction in the accomplishment of even menial tasks and that humility—applied as teachability and the search for truth—could be a higher power in disguise.

Then, unexpectedly, I was offered an executive job, involving many responsibilities. I could answer only, "I'll have to think about it."

Was I capable of staying sober? Was I really sober or only dry? Could I handle the responsibilities entailed and cope with renewed success? Or would God permit me to punish myself again?

I called a woman friend whom I was sponsoring. We talked it over, and she believed I could and should take the offer. Her faith reassured me; I knew the stimulation of being able to feel dignity again and gratification just to be alive. This newfound sense remained with me throughout the A.A. meeting we attended that evening. The subject under discussion was Step Eleven: "Sought through prayer and meditation to improve our conscious contact with God *as we understood Him*, praying only for knowledge of His will for us and the power to carry that out."

Home in the privacy of my room, I had another shock—a letter from my sister. I had seen her last in a sheriff's office, where she had regretfully ended the family's long effort to help me. "Even our prayers seem hopeless," she had said, "so I'll leave you to fend for yourself." Now came her letter, pleading to know where and how I was. Looking out the window at the soot and dirt of the rooftops and then inside at the meanness of my room, I thought with bitterness, "Yes indeed, if only they could see me now!" The saving grace was that I had nothing more to lose and naught to ask from anyone. Or had I?

All my youthful ideals had been washed away by alcohol. Now all the dreams and aspirations, family, position—everything I had once known—came back to jeer at me. I remembered hiding behind the trees in front of my former home to see my children go by the window; phoning my family just to hear familiar voices say, "Hello, hello—who's there?" before I hung up.

Sitting down on the bed, I picked up the letter and read it again and again. In my anguish, I could stand no more. Desperately, I cried, "Oh God, did You desert me? Or did I desert You?"

How much time went by, I don't know. Rising, I seemed to be drawn to the window. I beheld a transformation! The smut of that industrial city had disappeared under a covering of fresh snow. Everything was new and white and clean. Falling to my knees, I renewed that conscious contact with my God I had known as a boy. I didn't pray; I just talked. I didn't think; I just unburdened a heavy heart and a lost soul. I didn't thank; I only begged for help.

That night, finally at peace with myself for the first time in years, I slept the whole night through and awakened without fear and dread of another day. Continuing my prayer of the night before, I said, "I'll take the job. But, dear God, let's You and I play it together from now on."

While some days may offer only a modicum of frantic serenity, twenty-six years later I still know the same inner tranquillity that comes with forgiveness of self and the acceptance of God's will. Each new morning, there is faith in sobriety—sobriety not as mere abstinence from alcohol, but as progressive recovery in every facet of my life.

With my A.A. friend, my wife for twenty-five years now, I have joined my family for a joyous reunion. We know a contented and happy life, in which my sister and all the family share renewed and stronger bonds of affection. Since that day, I trust and am trusted.

Edmonton, Alberta

I WASN'T ALONE ANY MORE

I was in and around the Fellowship for three years, sometimes staying sober, sometimes cheating (myself, of course) a little or a lot. I loved A.A.—shook hands with everyone at every door at all meetings I attended, and they were many. I was a sort of A.A. hostess. Unfortunately, I still had a lot of trouble with *me*.

One member of my group used to say, "If you would just take the Third Step . . ." He might as well have been talking Dutch! I couldn't understand. Although I had been an honor student at Sunday school, I had gotten far away from anything spiritual.

At one point, I did manage to stay physically sober for six months. Then I lost my job and, at fifty-four, was sure I would never get another. Very frightened and depressed, I just couldn't face the future, and my stupid pride wouldn't allow me to ask anyone for help. So I went to the liquor store for my crutch.

In the next three and a half months, I died a hundred times. I still attended a lot of meetings when I could, but didn't tell anyone of my troubles. The other members had learned to leave me alone, because they felt helpless, and I understand now how they felt.

One morning, I awoke with a decision to stay in bed all day—that way I couldn't get a drink. I kept that decision, and when I got up at six, I felt secure, as the liquor stores closed at that hour. That night, I was desperately ill; I should have been in the hospital. About seven o'clock, I started to phone everyone I could think of, in and out of A.A. But no one could, or would, come to my aid. As a last effort, I phoned a blind man. I had worked and cooked for him for several years, and I asked him whether I could take a taxi and come to his apartment. I knew I was going to die, I told him, and I was afraid.

He said, "Die and be damned! I don't want you here." (He told me later he could have cut his tongue out, and thought of calling back. Thank God he didn't!)

I went to bed sure I would never get up again. My thinking had never been clearer. I couldn't really see any way out. By three o'clock in the morning, I still hadn't slept. I was propped up with pillows, and my heart was pounding almost out of my chest. My limbs started turning numb—first my legs above my knees, then my arms above my elbows.

I thought, "This is it!" I turned to the one source I had been too smart (as I saw it) or too stupid to appeal to earlier. I cried out, "Please, God, don't let me die like this!" My tormented heart and soul were in those few words. Almost instantly, the numbness started going away. I felt a Presence in the room. I wasn't alone any more.

God be praised, I have never felt alone since. I have never had another drink and, better still, have never needed one. It was a long way back to health, and it was quite a while before people had confidence in me. But that didn't really matter. *I* knew I was sober, and somehow I knew that, as long as I lived the way I believed God wanted me to live, I never need feel fear again.

Recently, I was told that I had a malignant tumor. Instead of being afraid or depressed, I thanked God for the past sixteen years of borrowed time He had given me. The tumor was removed; I feel fine and am enjoying every minute of every day. There will be many more days, I believe. As long as God has work for me to do, I will remain here.

Lac Carré, Quebec

A NEW MAN

I tried to help this man. It was a humiliating experience. No one enjoys being a complete failure; it plays havoc with the ego. Nothing seemed to work. I brought him to meetings, and he sat there in a fog, and I knew that only the body was present. I went to his home, and either he was out drinking or he sailed out the back door as I entered the front one. His family was beginning to enter a period of real hardship; I could feel their hopelessness.

Then came the hospital episode, the last in his extraordinary record of hospitalizations. He went into D.T.'s and convulsions, so violent that he had to be shackled to the bed. He was in a coma and being fed intravenously. Each day that I visited him, he looked worse, impossible as that seemed. For six days, he lay unconscious, unmoving except for the periodic shakes.

On the seventh day, I again visited him. Passing by his room, I noticed that the restraints had been removed and the intravenous feeding tubes had been taken away. I felt elated. He was going to make it! The doctor and the floor nurse dashed my hopes. He was slipping fast.

After I had arranged to have his wife brought there, it occurred to me that he was a Catholic and certain rites should be observed. It was a Catholic hospital, so I wandered down the hall and located a nun (the mother superior, it later turned out). She notified a priest and, with another nun, accompanied me back to the room.

While the priest entered the room alone, the three of us decided to sit on the bench in the corridor. Without any prearrangement, all three of us bowed our heads and began to pray—the mother superior, the nun, and I, a Presbyterian ordained deacon.

I have no way of telling how much time we spent there. I know the priest had left and gone about his other duties. What brought us back to the immediate present was a movement we heard from the room. When we looked in, the patient was sitting on the side of the bed!

"All right, God," he said. "I don't want to be the quarterback any more. Tell me what You want me to do, and I will do it."

The doctors later said that they had considered it physically impossible for him to move, much less sit up. And before this, he had not uttered a word since entering the hospital. The next statement he made was "I am hungry."

But the real miracle was what happened to him in the next ten years. He began helping people. I mean helping! No call has been too hard, too inconvenient, too "hopeless." He founded the A.A. group in his town, and he is embarrassed if you mention this to others or comment on the amount of A.A. work he is doing.

He is not the same man I was trying to twelfth-step. I failed in all my efforts to help the man I knew. And then Someone else provided a new man.

Bernardsville, New Jersey

FIGURE OF EVIL

It happened about three in the morning. I had been in our Fellowship slightly less than a year. I was alone in the house, my third wife having divorced me prior to my entry into A.A. I awoke with a frightening sense of approaching death. I was trembling and almost paralyzed with fear. Although it was in the month of August in Southern California, I was so cold that I found a heavy blanket and draped it around my shoulders. Then I turned on the floor heater in the living room and stood directly over it, trying to get warm. Instead of getting warm, I began to feel numb all over and again felt death approaching.

I had not been a very religious person, nor had I become affiliated with any church after coming into A.A. But suddenly I said to myself, "If ever I needed to pray, now is the time." I returned to the bedroom and fell to my knees at the side of the bed. I closed my eyes, buried my face in the palms of my hands, and rested my hands on the bed. I have forgotten all the words I said out loud, but I do recall saying, "Please, God, teach me to pray!"

Then, without raising my head or opening my eyes, I was able to "see" the entire floor plan of the house. And I could "see" a giant of a man standing on the other side of the bed, arms folded across his chest. He was glaring at me with a look of intense hatred and malevolence. He was the epitome of everything evil. After about ten seconds, I "saw" him slowly turn around, walk to the bathroom and look inside, turn to the second bedroom and look into it, walk to the living room and gaze around, then leave the house by way of the kitchen door.

I remained in my original position of prayer. Simultaneously with his departure, there seemed to be coming toward me from all directions, from the infinite reaches of space, a vibrating, pulsating, magnetic current. In probably fifteen seconds, this tremendous power reached me, stayed for some five seconds, and then slowly withdrew to its origin. But the sense of relief given me by its presence beggars description. In my clumsy way, I thanked God, got into bed, and slept like a baby.

I have not had the desire for a drink of anything intoxicating since that memorable morning twenty-three years ago. In my years in our Fellowship, I have had the privilege of hearing one other member describe an experience almost exactly like mine. Did the departure from my house of the personification of evil symbolize the departure from my life of the evils embraced by alcoholism, as some think? Be that as it may, the other part of my experience symbolizes to me the all-powerful and cleansing love of a Higher Power, whom I have since become happy to call God.

San Diego, California

DROWNING

Before my commitment to a state alcoholic center, I had had a dry stint in Alcoholics Anonymous. I know now that I had gone to A.A. to save my marriage, job, and liver, though no one could have convinced me at the time that I hadn't sought A.A. with all the proper motives. In seven months, my liver got well, and I got drunk for six weeks, winding up at the center.

On my eighth night there, I knew that I was dying. I was so weak that I could hardly breathe; my breath came in little gasps, quite far apart. If a drink had been put within an inch of my hand, I wouldn't have had the strength to take it. For the first time in my life, I was backed into a corner that I could not fight, cheat, lie, steal, or buy my way out of. I was trapped. For the first time in my life, I uttered a sincere prayer: "God, please help me." I didn't bargain with Him, nor did I suggest how or when He should help.

Immediately, I became calm and relaxed. There was no flash of lightning or clap of thunder, not even a still, small voice. I was scared. I didn't know what had happened. But I went to sleep and slept all night. When I awakened the next morning, I was refreshed, strong, and hungry. But the most wonderful thing was that, for the first time in my life, that dark, mysterious cloud of fear was gone. My first thought was to write to my wife about this experience, and I did. Imagine being able to write a letter after the condition I had been in the night before!

I am sure that some would classify this experience as an example of "letting go and letting God." Not this self-willed character! I had held on to the thin strand of my will until it just snapped, and then I was caught up by the "everlasting arms." I had to be rendered helpless, just like a drowning man who fights his rescuer.

I returned to A.A., but I was reluctant for a long time to tell of my experience. I was afraid that no one would believe me and that they would laugh. Later, I learned that others had had similar experiences.

A spiritual experience, I think, is what God does for a man when the man is completely helpless to do it for himself. A spiritual awakening is what a man does through his willingness to have his life transformed by following a proven program of spiritual growth, and this is a never-ending venture.

Raleigh, North Carolina

PRAYER 3

In A.A. we have found
that the actual good results of prayer
are beyond question. They are
matters of knowledge and experience. All those
who have persisted have found strength
not ordinarily their own. They have found
wisdom beyond their usual capability. And they
have increasingly found a peace of mind
which can stand firm in the face of
difficult circumstances.

Bill W.

"Twelve Steps and Twelve Traditions," page 104

INFINITE NEED

In practice, I have always found it rather difficult to let Allah's superior and flawless will prevail in my life and govern *my* will. However, when I make humble efforts, serenely accepting His will for me at some moment in my life, I feel absolutely relieved of the load I have carried on my shoulders. The mind does not wander any more, and the heart is full of happiness at every breath I take.

The most wonderful thing I have discovered is that prayer does work. I am beginning to think of Allah as a most loving Creator who is specially interested in me—otherwise, He would not have led me to A.A. nor given me so many chances to come out of slips. He is patient and merciful.

Although a moral inventory and a daily inventory reveal myriads of flaws in our makeups, still we, as human beings, cannot unravel *all* our liabilities in the personality. So at night, when I offer thanks to Him for the day's sobriety, I add a prayer: I ask Him to forgive my failings during the day, to help me to improve, and to grant me the wisdom to discover those faults in myself which I cannot lay my finger on.

In short, the need for prayer is infinite!

Karachi, Pakistan

MORE THAN A SYMBOL

In the not-too-distant days of my drunken past, when locomotion was failing and consciousness was fading, I would always manage to get at least one knee on the floor before I fell into bed. This gesture was accompanied by a mumbled "God, I'm checking in. I'm drunk." I tell this, not to elicit praise for having kept an outward vestige of the faith I knew as a child, but because I want to show the deep entrenchment of a symbol after the meaning was gone.

When my life was mercifully turned around and I threw in my lot with A.A.—because I could not do otherwise and live—a new prayer took the place of the old one. Monotonously, almost every moment when I was alone, I repeated, "God, please restore me to sanity."

And finally the answer began to come. A sane me was a startling revelation. Being able to look at the "what I was" part of my life with unclouded insight made me feel like a clairvoyant. I was looking into the life of someone I really had never known, though I knew everything that had taken place in her life. My perception is not keen enough to understand the how or why, but now at least I can see the pattern of that life.

Since my quiet miracle happened, when I happily found I did not need or want to drink, I have continued to pray. Now I say funny, private prayers, like one that is a line from a song, asking that there be peace on earth and that it begin with me. Most of my prayers are just short thank-yous for a favor or for making me stop to think before I act or react. My relationship with God has matured as any child's might normally do with his earthly father—I appreciate His kindness and wisdom more.

Nashville, Tennessee

"HOW DO YOU PRAY?"

Many times while I was drinking, I asked God to help me—and ended up calling Him all the curse names I could think of and saying, "If You're so almighty, why did You let me end up drunk and in all this trouble again?"

One day, I was sitting on the side of my bed, feeling all alone, with a shotgun shell in my hand, ready to load. "If there is a God," I cried out, "give me the courage to pull the trigger."

A voice, soft and very clear, spoke: "Get rid of that shell." I threw the shell out the door.

In a moment of calm, I dropped to my knees, and that voice spoke again: "Call Alcoholics Anonymous."

It startled me. I looked around, wondering where the voice came from, and I said out loud, "Oh God!" I jumped up and ran to the phone. As I grabbed for it, I knocked it to the floor. I sat down beside it and, with a shaking hand, dialed the operator and yelled for her to call A.A.

"I will connect you with information," she said.

"I'm shaking too damned bad to dial any numbers. You go to hell!"

I can't explain why I didn't hang up. I just sat there on the floor, with the receiver to my ear. The next thing I heard was "Good afternoon. Alcoholics Anonymous. May we help you?"

After I had been sober in A.A. four months, my wife and I got back together. I had always said it was her fault that I drank so much— all those crying kids and her complaining would cause anyone to drink. But after we had been back together for three months, I realized how wonderful a wife and mother she was. For the first time, I knew what real love was, instead of just using her.

Then it happened. I had always been afraid to love. For me, to love meant to lose. I believed that was God's way of punishing me for all the sins I had committed. My wife became very ill and was rushed to the hospital. She had cancer, a doctor finally told me. She might not pull through the operation, he said, and if she did, it would be only a matter of hours before she passed away.

I turned and ran down the hall. All I could think of was to get a bottle. I knew that if I got out the door, that's just what I would do. But a Power greater than myself caused me to stop and cry out, "My God, nurse! Call A.A.!"

I ran into the men's room and stayed there, crying, begging God to take me instead of her. Again the fear took over, and in self-pity I said, "Is this what I get for trying to work those damned Steps?"

I looked up, and the room was full of men, standing there looking at me. It seemed to me that they all stuck out their hands and said their names at the same time. "We're from A.A."

"Cry it all out," one of them said. "You'll feel better. And we understand."

I asked them, "Why is God doing this to me? I've tried so hard, and that poor woman—"

One of the men stopped me and said, "How do you pray?" I said that I asked God not to take her, but to take me. He then said, "Why don't you ask that God give you the strength and courage to accept His will? Say, 'Thy will, not mine, be done.'"

Yes, that was the first time in my life that I prayed for His will to be done. As I look back, I see that I had always asked God to do things *my* way.

I was sitting in the lobby with the A.A. men when two surgeons came up to me. One of them asked, "Can we talk to you in private?"

I heard myself answer, "Whatever you have to say, you can say it in front of them. They are my people."

The first doctor then spoke. "We have done all we can for her. She is still alive, and that is all we can say."

One of the A.A.'s put his arm around me and said to me, "Now why don't you turn her over to the greatest Surgeon of them all? Ask Him to give you the courage to accept." We all linked hands and joined in the Serenity Prayer.

How much time passed, I don't recall. The next thing I heard was a nurse speaking my name. She said softly, "You can see your wife now, but only for a couple of minutes."

As I ran up to the room, I thanked God for giving me this chance to let my wife know that I did love her and was sorry for my past. I was expecting to see a dying woman. To my surprise, my wife had a smile on her face and tears of joy in her eyes. She tried to reach out her arms, and in a weak voice she said, "You didn't leave me alone and go get drunk."

That was three years and four months ago. Today, we are still together. She works her program, Al-Anon, and I work mine, both of us living in today, one day at a time.

God answered my prayers, through the people of A.A.

Huntington Beach, California

GOD FOUND ME

I believe that God found me, more than I found Him. It was similar to watching a child walk; he falls down again and again, but it is better not to try to help him until he comes to realize that he cannot do it alone— and extends his hand. I had gotten myself into a position where I had no other place to turn; I was at a point of almost complete despair. Then, and only then, did I honestly and simply ask God to help me. He came to me instantly, and I could feel His presence, even as I do this moment.

Nashville, Tennessee

A SMALL WHITE CARD

When I came to A.A., I was a self-ordained atheist, a part-time agnostic, and a full-time antagonist—antagonistic toward everyone, everything in general, and God in particular. (This was due in part, I suppose, to my trying to hold on to my childhood concept of God.) A more bewildered, confused, powerless woman there never was. It seems that I had lost faith first in myself, then in other people, and finally in God. There was only one good thing about my refusal to believe that I had a Creator: It certainly relieved God of an embarrassing responsibility.

Yet I had a spiritual experience the night I called A.A., though I didn't realize it until later. Two angels came, carrying a real message of hope, and told me about A.A. My sponsor laughed when I denied that I had prayed for help. I told him that the only time I had mentioned God was when, in my despair at being unable to get either drunk or sober, I had cried out, "God! What am I going to do?"

He replied, "I believe that prayer was a pretty good one for a first one from an atheist. It got an answer, too." And so it did.

In a state more like rigor mortis than an acute hangover, I was taken to my first A.A. meeting, about sixty-five miles from my hometown. We visited a member's house on the way, and I caught my first glimpse of the Serenity Prayer, on a wall plaque. It was a shocker! I thought, "I've really got myself into another big mess with my drinking, as usual. I hope this prayer has nothing to do with A.A., for heaven's sake!" And I studiously avoided looking in that direction all afternoon.

Little did I know that, starting twenty-four hours later, the Serenity Prayer would be my companion and hope and salvation for five horrifying days and nights.

After we reached the closed A.A. meeting, in the evening, my whole attitude began to change in spite of myself. These people had something I lacked. And I wanted it! (Later, I learned that what they had was Power drive and Power steering, and that the source was a loving God as they understood Him.) They acted as if I was an answer to a prayer and they really wanted me there. (Eventually, the belief these A.A.'s had in me led me to believe in them, then in myself again, and finally in God.)

One of the women handed me a small white card with the Serenity Prayer printed on it. "What if I don't believe in God?" I asked.

She grinned and said, "Well, I believe that He believes in you. Didn't you say that you were willing to go to any lengths?" And she added, "Just hang on to this card for dear life! If you're tempted to take that first drink, read it. Or read it if you run into some other problem too big for you to handle."

At home, just twenty-four hours later, I did begin hanging on to that little card "for dear life." My husband of twenty-five years went into D.T.'s. In his madness, he prevented me from phoning or going for help. For five days and nights, there was no sleep for either of us, and there were times when I became part of his nightmares and my life was threatened.

All the while, I never allowed the card to leave my person. I read and reread the Serenity Prayer. Though the house was as well stocked with liquor as a small bar, the miracle of it all was that I did not take a drink! Me!—who had solved all my problems with strong drink. Instead, I clutched that little card and murmured the words over and over for five days and nights. I do not recall making any decision to believe. I felt only that the God of these A.A. people might take pity on me and help me. But I certainly had come to believe that *I* was powerless. As our Big Book states, "The alcoholic at certain times has no effective mental defense against the first drink. Except in a few rare cases, neither he nor any other human being can provide such a defense. His defense must come from a Higher Power."

All this so soon after my first meeting! The whole experience caused me to listen intently to other members' stories of how they came to believe; it caused me to read and reread the chapter "We Agnostics" in the Big Book and the words on the same subject in "Twelve Steps and Twelve Traditions." At last, I came to the conclusion that there *was* "an easier, softer way"—easier than anything I had tried for myself before A.A. I came to believe.

And lest I forget . . . I still have in my possession a small, tattered, faded Serenity Prayer card, which saved my sanity and my sobriety and restored my faith in the God of my understanding.

Brighton, Colorado

HEARD AT MEETINGS

"Many people pray as though to overcome the will of a reluctant God, instead of taking hold of the willingness of a loving God."

"It is wise to pray for the future, but not to worry about it, because we can't live it until it becomes the present. The depth of our anxiety measures the distance we are from God."

"If we have the opportunity to help in some practical way when our loved ones or other people we are concerned about are in trouble—let's do so. If there is no such opportunity, let's pray for them and believe that, in so doing, we are helping to connect their minds to God's influence. But let's not expect same-day service. The important part is not to cancel our prayers by later worrying. (There is a vast difference between being concerned and worrying.) Long-distance, unconditional faith is the best kind."

Sydney, Australia

RELEASE
FROM
OBSESSION
4

*In the late stages
of our drinking, the will to resist
has fled. Yet when we admit complete
defeat and when we become entirely ready
to try A.A. principles, our obsession
leaves us and we enter a new
dimension—freedom under God
as we understand Him.*

Bill W.

Letter, 1966

TOTAL SURRENDER

What has always impressed me most about the program and myself is the constant, continuing challenge to try recapturing some of the true and honest rapture I felt upon total surrender, when I first came into A.A. For me, that special peace of mind has never been duplicated. Now, after all the accumulated twenty-four-hour periods, I realize that it probably never will be. I have come close to it a few times, but it's never the same.

I think there is a relationship between that feeling and our need at the time we were introduced to the program. Our motivation, I believe, is a combination of enough hurt and the grace of God. Surely a strange combination! I would not know how to express it to anyone outside A.A.

Des Plaines, Illinois

HE TOOK CONTROL

I could not believe sobriety would benefit me. With a working wife, a beautiful home, a big, impressive automobile, and credit cards in my pocket, who needed help? I could not believe there would be any fun in life without booze, nightclubs, and honky-tonk angels. I could not believe "those rummies" in A.A. were as interested in my welfare as they claimed to be. And I certainly couldn't believe that people who admitted having spent time in the funny farm could show *me* a better way of life.

Nor did I need them to tell me about God. My grandmother, my aunts, and many other people had tried that. Although not caring to be called a Christian, I did believe there was a God of some sort, somewhere, who would help me if I really needed outside help. But I was man enough and smart enough to help myself! So I wasn't asking God, or anyone else, for help.

In those last three years, while playing revolving door with the Fellowship, I drank up all my excuses for not needing A.A. One evening, I sat alone in my apartment, counting my bankroll—eighty-nine cents. There was no food in my apartment. Should I spend eighty-five cents for another bottle of wine?

Yes, I had to! It would be impossible for me to face the world in the morning without a drink. But, then, I really didn't have to face the world in the morning, because I no longer had a job to go to, nor a wife to nag at me, nor kids to badger me for school money.

What could I do? My mind became hopelessly weary at this point and refused even to attempt a decision. Desperately, hoping He might be listening, I knelt beside my empty wine bottle and prayed very simply, "Oh God, please help me."

The answer came immediately. I knew I could somehow get through the night—and even face the morning light—without another bottle.

The next day, I went to a rehabilitation house for alcoholic men. During my stay, attending A.A. meetings daily and talking about alcoholism and sobriety with people whose personal sobriety ranged from one day to twenty-five years, I came to believe.

The Higher Power had taken away, for that one night, my constant craving for alcohol, and He had guided me back to A.A. But the craving for booze came back to me. I had to fight it constantly, even though I was sincerely trying to work the A.A. program. When the Steps were read, "God *as we understood Him*" bothered me. These people had something I was unable to grasp. I had never been able to understand God, and still didn't. Changing His name to "Higher Power" didn't help any.

One of the oldtimers used the electricity metaphor, which I later found in the Big Book. "A person walking into a dark room does not worry about understanding electricity," he said. "He just finds the switch and turns on the light." He explained that we can turn on the switch of spirituality by simply asking God each morning for another day of sobriety and thanking Him at night for another beautiful sober day. He said, "Do it mechanically if you really don't believe in it. But do it every day. There is probably no one who really understands the wonderful ways of the Higher Power, and we don't need to. He understands us."

So I prayed every morning and night. Sometimes I meant it; sometimes I didn't. I got a job, because I was no longer afraid to ask for one. It was not the type of job to be proud of, and the paycheck was small. However, it made me self-supporting, and I moved from the rehab to a little apartment.

One Saturday evening, my pity-pot got too big for me, and I fell in. Here was I, two months sober, trying so hard to work the program. Being so honest that it hurt. Continually fighting that physical craving for a drink. And what had it gotten me? Nothing. Living alone in a dingy place. Working at a job I despised. Earning barely enough to spare a quarter for the "no fees" basket.

To hell with it—I might as well be drunk! Heading for the territory I had favored during the latter period of my bar drinking, I unconsciously made three wrong turns—on streets I know as you know your own living room—and wound up at an A.A. club. I was out of the car and up on the porch before realizing I had driven the wrong way.

Well, I'd go in and say goodbye. . . . Somehow, I wound up going to a nearby meeting with two A.A. friends, and the meeting was so good that it completely washed the bar-hopping idea out of my mind.

When I walked into my apartment and flipped the light switch, another light came on. A light inside my thick skull!

That night, I fervently thanked the God I did not understand for taking complete control of my mind and body long enough to deliver me to my A.A. friends, thereby saving me from "one drunk too many." Then and there, I came to believe that God could and would do for me what no human power could. Since that time, I have not had a craving for a drink of alcohol. Since that time, I have come to believe that anything relevant to a better life is made possible by daily living the A.A. way with the help of an understanding God, whom I still do not understand.

San Diego, California

"UNDER GOD"

The desire to drink was removed and never returned once I accepted Step Three—during a terrific storm in the North Pacific. After all, *you* don't have much to say about it. Lloyd's of London's definition of a master of a ship is "captain under God."

A.A. Internationalists

A NEW FEELING

Since childhood, I have believed in God, but I quit going to church when the booze took over. For eleven years, I did not have a sober day, except a few times when I was hospitalized or under a doctor's care. I prayed many times, but I felt I was not getting through to God.

One day toward the end of those years, I made the mistake of mixing liquor with medication given me by my neighborhood doctor. My wife was sure I was dead. The next day, the doctor said that if his phone had been tied up for just minutes when she called, he would have been too late—my heartbeat and pulse were gone when he arrived. Still, after two weeks of recovery in the hospital and then eight more weeks on the wagon, I began drinking again. Within two months, I reached a point where I wanted to die and could not.

Down in Texas, my sister had met an A.A., and after receiving a letter from her, I agreed to get in touch with a member in my town. I would have bet ten dollars to a plugged nickel it was a false alarm, but I did go to meet him. He lent me his Big Book and advised me to try to read it with a clear head and meet him the following Thursday night and attend an A.A. meeting.

I told my wife that I had never talked to a man who seemed to understand my problem as he did. About seven p.m., I went into the bathroom, to the medicine cabinet where I kept my liquor, and took a drink from a pint I had just bought. Now I was ready to read the A.A. book. After reading about an hour, I automatically got up to get another drink. But I stopped, remembering I had promised to read with a clear head. So I postponed the drink and kept on reading.

When I came to the chapter "We Agnostics," I read: "We needed to ask ourselves but one short question. 'Do I now believe, or am I even willing to believe, that there is a Power greater than myself?' " This impressed me very much.

All the same, I went to the bathroom to take one big drink before retiring, as I had done every night for years. As I reached for the bottle, the thought occurred to me that—just maybe—if I asked God for a little help, He might hear me. I turned out the light, and for the first time in my life I talked to God with all honesty and sincerity: "Dear God, if You will, listen to me. I am, as You know, absolutely no good to my family, my friends, and myself. This liquor has beaten me down to the ground, and I am unable to do anything about it. Now, if You will, let me get a night's rest without this drink."

I went to bed. The first thing I knew, it was six-thirty a.m., time to get up. When I sat on the side of the bed, for the first time in years I did not have the cold sweats and shakes. I decided I must have gotten up and drunk some more liquor in the early morning hours. But no— the bottle was there, just as I had left it the night before.

I shaved without having to take on six or eight ounces of liquor first. I went out into the kitchen and told my wife about this change and the new feeling I had. I even drank a cup of coffee holding the cup with one hand, instead of pouring it into a bowl and holding it with both hands. "If God *is* helping me," I said, "I sure hope He keeps on." She said He would if I tried to help myself.

Thursday night, I did meet the A.A. man, and we attended my first meeting, and I met the finest and most understanding people I had ever known. I was forty-three then. I am now seventy-one. I can honestly say that I have never even come close to a slip, and with God as my silent partner, I am sure I can make it another twenty-four hours.

Evansville, Indiana

"USE ME"

After joining A.A. in October, I drank on Christmas Day and again on New Year's Eve, and no disaster followed. I returned to my A.A. group feeling as smug as anything, because I had survived the holidays. I would lick this thing yet. It hadn't gotten the better of *me*!

Two weeks later, I was suddenly taken drunk. I hadn't planned it; I hadn't even thought about it; I just started drinking, and I couldn't seem to stop until I passed out. Something was wrong with me. I was sick with a sickness that went deep into my very soul. I couldn't stand myself. I couldn't look my children in the face. I couldn't face anything.

I dragged myself back to the A.A. group. And I *listened*, and I heard for the first time. That night, I returned to my home in a state of numbness. I was up against something I didn't know how to cope with. My luck wasn't going to change. *I* was going to have to change. But could I? God, as I understood Him, surely was disgusted with me by now. I had bargained and cajoled and broken every promise that I had ever made to Him. How could I turn to Him now?

As I sat in that empty room, I could hear the words "For God so loved the world . . . For God *so loved* the world . . ."

The words that I finally uttered seemed to have been wrung from me: "Oh, dear God, where am I going to find the strength to overcome my alcoholism?"

The voice that answered was calm and sweet beyond description. "You have the strength. All you have to do is use it. I am here. I am with you. Use *Me*."

I was born again that day. From that moment, the compulsion was lifted. In the eleven years since, I have found in sobriety what I was searching for in the bottle. I wanted peace; God gave me peace. I wanted acceptance; God accepted me. I wanted to be loved; God assured me that He loved me.

My children are grown now, and they are beautiful children, who daily, routinely practice the principles of the A.A. program—love and service and honesty. We all grew up together, and that makes us good friends.

Honolulu, Hawaii

STAY SOBER ON LOVE

I had been around A.A. for almost two years and had had little success at staying sober. One day, I found myself in a small room in downtown Toronto, having drunk myself out of the love and respect of a lovely wife, four healthy children, a mother, a father, other relatives, and friends. I was alone once again, with those terrible feelings of complete isolation and fear of impending doom. So once again, filled with hate, envy, lust, slothfulness, and, most of all, total hopelessness, I presented myself at the doors of Alcoholics Anonymous.

My A.A. friends were somewhat skeptical about my return to the fold—justifiably, having watched me bounce around and put together only six months of continuous sobriety. But I thank God for the compassion, the love, and the understanding of an A.A. husband-and-wife team, who helped me to live and breathe A.A. for the next forty-five days, through telephone conversations, open meetings, discussion meetings, long talks at the kitchen table, and, most important, prayer.

I had mocked the spiritual aspect of our program on many previous occasions, claiming that this God business was for sissies and hypocrites. But this time it was different. After my last drunk, I knew that it would be death or insanity for me if I kept on drinking. This time, I prayed. I somehow felt that if there *was* a Power greater than myself who could relieve me of this suffering, then I had better try to find Him.

On my forty-fifth day of new sobriety, I returned to the small room in downtown Toronto and sank into a depression that no words can describe. It was as if my body and my soul were completely divided. I saw, as clearly as I will ever see, the complete futility of my existence and the destruction brought about by my stubborn, prideful delusion that I could have "just a few." I had reached a point in life where I could not go on alone, drunk or sober. That, my friends, was a loneliness I hope I never forget.

A very strange thing happened to me that afternoon. I refused to give in and take a drink. After almost three hours of agony, I cried out for God's help. And I left the room with a strength that I had never thought it possible to attain.

For the next two weeks, I felt "turned on," with no booze and no other drugs. For the first time in my adult life, I was unmistakably aware of the living presence of God within myself and the universe. Seeing the beauty in a child's face or green grass or a tree and feeling the joy of waking up in the morning with a clear head, looking forward to the day's activities, were new and wonderful experiences. The resentments, the hates, the fears all seemed to be lifted; I was able to forgive and forget.

The things I thought I needed for so many years no longer seem important, now that I have become aware of the spiritual resources God has given me. With these, I don't need alcohol to function. What a joy to stay sober on love instead of fear!

Since that time, I have enjoyed some seventeen months of sobriety. I write this for the alcoholic who feels he or she has gone too far against God's will in actions, words, and deeds ever to get well again. If you are sincere in your prayers, this wonderful gift is available to you, as it was to me.

Toronto, Ontario

"ASK GOD FOR STRENGTH"

My parents provided a wholesome atmosphere for my upbringing, offered me a good education, and took me to their church. But their concept of a fearsome, revengeful God was a threat to me, and I tried to stay far away from Him and His believers. Yet the need for the approval of my family and friends was in conflict with my disbelief. Unable to live up to my parents' teaching, I ran and ran, denying myself a belief in God.

When I came into A.A. in 1955, I was only thirty-one. "You are too young. You haven't drunk enough. You haven't suffered enough," some members said. I still had my family (though it was a second one), a job, and a bank account, and I was buying a home. All the same, I had hit a high bottom, a low bottom, and all the bottoms in between. So I attended A.A. meetings, and for five months I awaited the striking of a thunderbolt that would transform this young man into a responsible, recovered alcoholic. My vision, however, was limited; my hearing, dulled. The disappointment of not experiencing a great spiritual reawakening caused me to relax my efforts to recover; but after each bout with the bottle, I always returned to A.A.

I had four good sponsors. One was my spiritual adviser, with whom I felt little empathy. Each time he stood at the podium, he spoke of God as he understood Him. While I resented the references and listened against my will, one day he struck a responding chord. He said, "When you have used up all resources of family, friends, doctors, and ministers, there is still one source of help. It is one that never fails and never gives up, and is always available and willing."

These words returned to me one morning, at the end of a three-week binge in a hotel room. I was acutely aware of the shambles my life had become. Now my second marriage was on the rocks, and the children were being hurt. That morning, I was able to be honest. I knew I had failed as a father, husband, and son. I had failed at school and in the service and had lost every job or business I had tried. Neither religion, the medical profession, nor A.A. had succeeded with me. I felt completely defeated. Then I remembered some of the words of my sponsor: "When all else has failed, grab a rope and hang on. Ask God for strength to stay sober for one day."

I went into the filthy bathroom and got down on my knees. "God, teach me to pray," I begged. I remained there a long time, and when I arose and left the room, I knew I never had to drink again. I came to believe, that day, that God would help me maintain my sobriety. Since then, I've come to believe that He will help me with any problem.

During the years since my last drink, I haven't encountered as many problems as before. As I grow more capable of understanding the things that have happened to me, I don't think it was on that morning in the hotel that I found God. I think He had been within me at all times, just as He is in all people, and I uncovered Him by clearing away the wreckage of my past, as the Big Book recommends.

Birmingham, Alabama

SHATTERED GLASS

"It was the best of times, it was the worst of times . . ." With these words begins Charles Dickens's novel "A Tale of Two Cities." In my life, 1968 was just such a year. As it opened, every move was driving me nearer to despair. My family had long since ceased to say anything to me except that they hoped I would find myself soon. Fortunately, they let me work it out alone. Few alcoholics have this chance. I could have been brought home and hidden, committed to an institution, or told I was no good and abandoned. Instead, love and faith in a Higher Power told my family to watch and wait.

My first call to A.A. was to have some literature sent. When it came, I devoured every word and continued to drink. Finally, I called

A.A. again. I was afraid to call home to ask to be sent to an institution, though I was convinced I was insane; no sane person would continue to drink if she didn't want to.

For about three months, I attended meetings four times a week. Rewarding as each encounter with the program was, there still seemed to be a large loophole in my achieving the serenity we prayed for so often. (During this time, the Big Book was not mentioned to me.) One evening, in a very low mood, I poured myself a drink. It seemed as if someone else were acting in my place. I dropped the glass.

As I poured another drink, I found I was praying for help. The second glass fell and shattered as the first had. Undaunted, I poured another, held on to it with both hands, and drained it. Suddenly, it became clear that this was not what I wanted.

Fear trembled to the surface, and I raced to the phone and shakily dialed the number of a new A.A. friend. She came at once and spent the entire evening with me. We discussed the First Step, and I felt at home with the words. When we got to the Second Step, I admitted complete confusion. Late that night, she left me with those 575 pages of inspiration called the Big Book.

I sat down at once to read. About Chapter Four, the word "hope" sprang from the pages with the vividness of neon. I read and reread the sentences until I realized that laughter and tears were intermixed and I was no longer seated, but pacing around the room like a madwoman. It was as if a great load had been lifted from my shoulders. For the first time, I began to understand that I couldn't drink like other people, that I wasn't like other people, and that I no longer had to try to be. I felt like Scrooge in another Dickens classic, "The Christmas Carol," when he awakes to discover he hasn't missed Christmas after all. He dances, cries, and laughs aloud, just as I was doing. Scrooge and I had been reborn to live life as we had never known it.

The crest of this experience lasted several hours. When I fell into an exhausted sleep, it was with the knowledge that I had at last begun my adjustment to life as an alcoholic. From that moment, things seemed to change from within. Gradually, I could recognize when I was getting in my own way, and I could step aside, for "Thy will, not mine" had become more than mere words. There have been many times when this revelation has been hard to hold on to, but, little by little, it seems easier every day. My course has become two steps forward, one step backward, two more forward, instead of always complete retreat. The days are too short, and they are seldom dull. Each day is a new challenge to stay sober and to keep moving straight ahead.

Charleston, West Virginia

A SPIRITUAL AWAKENING 5

*Is sobriety all that we
are to expect of a spiritual awakening?
No, sobriety is only a bare beginning;
it is only the first gift of the
first awakening. If more gifts are to be
received, our awakening has to go on.
As it does go on, we find that bit by bit
we can discard the old life—the one
that did not work—for a new life that can
and does work under any conditions
whatever.*

Bill W.

LETTING GO

For a long time, I had the idea that I must succeed, I must be right, I must be important. If I let go, I thought, then I wouldn't be anybody. Well, who was I, anyway? Just a willful alcoholic woman.

Now I'm beginning to see that letting go doesn't mean giving up. It means opening myself to new vistas. There have been moments of what I would call ecstasy. I'm thrilled and I'm scared at the same time. I feel, "I'd better not enjoy this, because it is going to go away." It's so hard for me to say, "Okay, you've had a little insight. Just let it happen!"

The A.A. program says, "Look, we've got some things to give you that are really going to help—if you'll slow down long enough and if you'll relax."

These are not things that are going to make me special or get me a better job or make me important. They are just going to offer me a way of life that is beautiful. When I say, "I want to know something about the spirit in me," you say, "Go ahead. There isn't anything to be afraid of. The darkness you may encounter isn't going to last, because there will always be somebody to help you."

San Francisco, California

ACTION AND PATIENCE

In common with many A.A.'s, I never enjoyed the luxury of a large and conscious spiritual experience, and I felt a little deprived. But "We have a better program than we know," as Bill, our co-founder, said. I came to believe by way of that program, though I have recognized the process only in retrospect.

I had started with an optimistic, idealized view of life, supported by a strong religious commitment and faith. Somewhere along the way,

I became a victim of the "sickness unto death"—alienated, anxious, alone. I found myself in the midst of a journey into darkness, separated from God, from other people, from my own being. I regret many things that happened on this journey, but I no longer regret that it took place. Some of us are more blinded by our pride and willfulness than others, and have to be broken in order to see.

I had to realize that of myself I had no power to help myself. The day came, by the grace of God, when I had that "moment of truth," though at the time I experienced it more as a plunge into deeper darkness than as the "leap of faith" which it ultimately proved to be, more as a humiliating defeat than as the transforming experience of my life.

In shame and despair, I went to my first A.A. meeting. By some minor miracle, I was able to suspend opinion, analysis, judgment, and criticism, and instead to listen and hear. I heard someone say that A.A. works for those who work for it, those who put *action* into the program. For me, at that time, action consisted of simply showing up at an A.A. meeting and following the suggestions I heard. I heard that I should forget about yesterday and tomorrow and instead concentrate on today and staying away from the first drink today—now. I tried it, and it worked. The first step in the process of "coming to believe" had been taken.

I heard this action had to be backed up with *patience*, that in time, for instance, I would sleep without the sedation of alcohol. Each night, after the A.A. meeting, I surrounded myself with books and magazines and ginger ale and sat down before the television set, prepared to stay awake all night. This was action for me at that time—following instructions. I was prepared to wait for sleep. I didn't have to wait long. For the first time in memory, I fell asleep in a chair before the television set, and I came to believe a little more.

I heard that we can't keep what we have unless we give it away. And so I found a woman—someone a little newer than I was—and I shared with her what you had shared with me. Looking back on it, I doubt that I helped this woman very much, but I helped myself beyond measure. I stayed sober, day by day, through sharing my experience, strength, and hope with her, through putting *action* into the A.A. program—while, at the same time, waiting for her, not forcing my action on her. This was *patience* supporting the action, though I didn't call it patience at the time; the word was not a part of my emotional vocabulary.

As time went on, my life became totally involved in A.A. action. I had experienced the power of God's forgiveness, and, through grace, I was able to make this response of gratitude that is beyond verbal expression. God's grace had overcome the death that was in me and instead had made me a member of the "society of the second chance." If this grace had been contingent on my righteousness or obedience or goodness or sacrifice, as acts of the will, it would never have come to me, because I had none of these things going. It was an unearned favor to an unlikely prospect. This grace that overcomes death by forgiveness is the truth that has set me free to regard myself and you as acceptable, because God accepts us for what we are—imperfect creatures. And if, as I pray, I should continue to grow in grace, it will be through love and service to this Fellowship and to the Power greater than myself that I call God.

New York, New York

AN UNKNOWN PLAN

I did believe until about the age of thirteen, when my mother passed away, leaving me an orphan (I had lost my father when I was four). I had attended Sunday school; I had gone to church regularly with my mother; I had joined the church at age twelve. I can remember the stories my mother and Sunday-school teachers told about God, Jesus, and heaven, also those about the Devil and his house of hell.

After Mother died, two older brothers and I made our home with an uncle and aunt. For a while, I went on attending church services regularly, but I could not understand why my mother had been taken away, and the feeling of doubt started in; church and Sunday school were neglected.

I had my first drink in my teens, and from that day until the day I joined A.A., alcohol was in, and God and church began to go out. My doubt and disbelief increased until there was no God or heaven, Devil or hell so far as I was concerned. With the bottle, this kind of thinking seemed easy and right. I could have committed murder in a blackout and felt no guilt, no sense of wrongdoing whatever. There is no way for me to put in words the size of my resentment.

At last, sure that no one cared for me, knowing that I cared for no one, I decided to do something permanent about this thing called life—exterminate it. I placed a shotgun against my chest and pulled the trigger.

When I was taken to the hospital, the doctors stated (I was told later), "This man should have been dead hours ago." Can you imagine what they had being called a *man*? For days, I was in a coma with no hope for survival, according to the doctors and nurses. At times, I would come to for a fleeting second, and then I believed once more in hell and its owner, the Devil. I could not believe that I was alive.

I do not know how many times this coming to and relapsing into a coma occurred; but eventually there was a moment when I recognized people in the room. Some time later, I realized that I actually was alive. Still later, I began to believe that something greater than I was had taken over. At that time, I could not associate this "something" with God; it was just something greater. But I could have told my doctors and nurses that I was going to get well, because a power greater than they were or I was had a plan. We were only tools in that plan, I felt; I had no idea what it was; I asked only that it be revealed.

A.A. came to me, in the person of a member, while I was in the hospital. After I was released, several A.A.'s took me to a rehabilitation center. When I had completed the program there, I returned to my hometown and was welcomed into the local A.A. group. I found a part-time job—from one hour up to a full day, as my physical condition would permit, according to the doctor's advice. This behavior was not like people I had known, and it was completely out of line with me. Work! For years, all I had known was drink, gamble, and drink, plus all that goes with that kind of living.

One day, after an hour at work, I had to leave. My boss took me home, to the A.A. clubhouse where I lived and had been appointed houseman, and this is what happened.

I was sitting in the most comfortable chair available, looking at the Twelve Steps and Traditions hanging on the wall, reading them over, with a little better understanding each time. The coffee was beginning to smell like it needed tasting, and that's what I did. Now the payoff. Something drew me back to the chair and my eyes to the Twelve Steps. I got the message—the meaning—like a flash of lightning. I recognized the Power whose presence I had felt in the hospital: God, as I understand Him. And the plan was revealed to me: ". . . to carry this message to alcoholics . . . to practice these principles in all our affairs."

There's quite a difference between the person who did not believe, had no God, and wanted to die—and the person of today, who came to believe, is not afraid of dying, but wants to live. I've got a lot of message-carrying to do!

Stuttgart, Arkansas

NEW SELVES UNFOLDING

In my own experience, a spiritual awakening was not *found*, by seeking it. Others claimed spiritual belief came with sobriety, and I wanted that belief so desperately that I almost missed it altogether.

Then a series of adversities set in. It seemed everything I had was swept away. My emotional stability was so tested that a couple of times I considered suicide.

But at no time was a drink considered, even though craving for the taste of liquor hit me momentarily at times. However, the First Step and I have always been great friends. I repeated it every five seconds and thanked God each day for my sobriety—the only grace, maybe, for that day.

Gradually, I began to see another part of me emerging—a grateful me, expecting nothing, but sure that another power was beginning to guide me, counsel me, and direct my ways. And I was not afraid.

Then, as this power began to unfold new selves within me, a greater understanding of my fellowmen began. With a new awakening each day—new strengths, new truths, new acceptance of A.A. people and people not in A.A.—a new world opened up. And every day it still does.

The adversities, loneliness, sickness, losses, and disappointments mean nothing now. I'm happy, because I came to believe—not only in God, but in the goodness in everyone.

Barberton, Ohio

ON A WINTER DAY

Nearly nine months had passed since I had taken a drink, and I was miserable. My wife and I attended A.A. meetings regularly, and I'd sit there cursing the "happy hypocrites" who were enjoying themselves and their sobriety. I felt sorry for myself because I had no job. (Of course, the type I wanted was at least the vice-presidency of a large firm.)

This particular day had dawned clear and cold, following one of the worst snow and ice storms Atlanta had experienced in many years. Trees, poles, and power and telephone lines were down everywhere; ice and snow blanketed everything in sight. As I moped around the house, my thoughts turned to the previous summer, when I had escaped the misery that surrounded me by helping with the Little League baseball team. I hadn't given much time or thought to my son until after A.A., and I was pleased when he asked me to take him to play with the Little League. The team coach turned out to be a man I had played ball with when we were kids, and he asked me about helping out with the team. Naturally, I was delighted.

That summer, we lost a little boy in our league. He was cycling home from the ball park, and a drunk driver ran him off the road and knocked him from his bicycle. When his head hit the curb, he was killed. This boy so loved the Little League that his parents asked and readily received permission to bury him in his uniform. They bought a lot on a hill in the cemetery overlooking the Little League ball park and buried Jimmy there, facing the field.

This icy morning, I got into my car and drove up that cemetery hill as far as I could go, then got out and walked the rest of the way to Jimmy's grave. This was one of the most beautiful days I have ever seen in my life. Not a twig was moving; the sky was clear blue; the quiet was disturbed only when a little dog ran across Jimmy's grave—and I thought Jimmy would have liked that.

As I stood there beside his tombstone, I remembered an old favorite hymn of mine, "In the Garden." Standing there, I felt God's hand was on my shoulder, and we had a wonderful visit of meditation together.

Then a sense of guilt and shame came over me. I had been a drunk. All I had to do was take one drink, and I could put another little Jimmy on the side of some hill like this one. I wouldn't have to stay drunk for a month or a week or a day; all I had to do was to take one drink, and I would be capable of killing a child.

I knew I had to have a new beginning, and this beginning had to be here. I could not start anywhere else. I had to let go of the past and forget the future. As long as I held on to the past with one hand and grabbed at the future with the other hand, I had nothing to hold on to today with. So I had to begin here, now.

The next time I went back to my A.A. group, the "happy hypocrites" looked different to me. I began to see love in their eyes, a greater warmth than I had ever seen before. I mentioned it to my sponsor, and he said, "The reason you see love in these people's eyes is because you are beginning to love them. The love that we see in their eyes is the reflection of our own love. We have got to love to be loved."

Decatur, Georgia

"THE BELIEF WILL COME"

In the beginning, I rejected any part of the A.A. program that referred to God in any manner. I even remained silent when they closed the meetings with the Lord's Prayer. (I didn't know the words, anyhow.)

Looking back, I don't think I was an agnostic, nor do I think I was an atheist. But I do know this: I couldn't accept any of "the God bit," nor did I want to come to believe or have any spiritual awakening.

After all, I had come to A.A. to get sober, and what did all this truck have to do with that?

Even with all my stupid arrogance, you still loved me, held out your hand of friendship, and, I'm sure, used cautious wisdom in trying to reach me with the program. But I could hear only what I wanted to hear.

I remained dry for a number of years, and then, as you may already have guessed, I drank again. It was inevitable. I had accepted only those parts of the program that fitted into my life without effort on my part. I was still the self-centered egotist I had always been, still full of all my old hatreds, selfishness, and disbelief—just as lacking in maturity as I had been when I first arrived at A.A.

This time, when I came to in the hospital, I had absolutely no hope. After all, you had told me that A.A. was the last hope for the alcoholic, and I had failed—there was nothing else. At this very point, my sister chose to send me a clipping from a Sunday-school paper. No letter, just the clipping: "Pray with disbelief; but pray with sincerity; and the belief will come."

Pray? How could I pray? I didn't know how to pray. Still, I was ready to go to any lengths to get my sobriety and some semblance of a normal life. I guess I just gave up. I stopped fighting. I accepted that which I did not really believe, much less understand.

I started praying, not in any formal way. I just talked to God or, rather, cried out, "Dear God, help me. I'm a drunk." I had nowhere left to turn, except to this God I did not know.

I don't recall any immediate, dramatic change in my life. I do recall telling my wife how hopeless it all seemed. At her suggestion, I began rereading the Big Book and the Twelve Steps, and now I found in these much that I had never found before. I didn't reject any of it. I accepted it just as it was written. Nor did I read anything into it that wasn't there.

Again, nothing changed overnight. But, as time has passed, I have acquired a blind and, yes, childlike faith that, by accepting a God I don't understand and the program of A.A. just as it is written, I can maintain my sobriety one day at a time. If I am to have more than this, it will come as time goes by, just as other good things have come.

I no longer find it necessary, as I did for years, to prove my disbelief in God by my every thought and deed. Nor do I find it necessary to prove myself to others. No—the only accounting and the only proving I have to do is to myself and to God, as I understand Him (or don't understand Him). I'm sure that I shall err from time to time, but I must learn to forgive myself, as God has forgiven me for my past.

I think I have had a spiritual awakening, as undramatic as it may have been, and that it will go on and on as long as I continue to practice this program in my daily affairs. To me, there is no "spiritual side" to the program of Alcoholics Anonymous; the entire program is spiritual.

In my view, some of the evidences of a spiritual awakening are: maturity; an end to habitual hatred; the ability to love and to be loved in return; the ability to believe, even without understanding, that Something lets the sun rise in the morning and set at night, makes the leaves come out in the spring and drop off in the fall, and gives the birds song. Why not let this Something be God?

St. Petersburg, Florida

ON A BIG SCREEN

I drank for about twenty-eight years, starting out as a social drinker, becoming a periodic drunk, then a compulsive drinker. My drinking cost me my home, my first wife, my children, and just about everything I had ever worked for all my life. I was arrested for being drunk in public; I developed TB, and I knew that my heavy drinking had probably brought it on; in four months, I was in and out of four alcoholic wards in different hospitals. On my release from the last one, I stayed drunk for three solid weeks—and woke up in jail again. I thought I was there, as before, for being drunk in public. But after asking, I found that I had committed a felony.

On a cold morning, I entered the penitentiary to begin a five-year sentence. After being processed and taken to my cell in the receiving unit and hearing that iron door slam behind me, I thought this was the end for me. I had gone just about as far down as I could go, and I felt there was no hope.

In the next five weeks, I sat in that small cell and blamed everyone but myself for all my past and present troubles. No one could be more full of resentment, hate, and self-pity than I was at that time.

One night, while I was in my cell looking at the four walls, my whole past life seemed to open up before me, as if on a big screen. I could plainly see for the first time all the heartaches and misery and pain that I had brought on everyone in the past: my mother and father, my first wife and my children, my present wife, and all my friends. For the first time, I realized none of these people were wrong. I was the one who was wrong. All of the things that had happened to me, I had brought on myself while drinking. I believe this moment was the first time I had been honest with myself in many years.

Soon after that, I received a letter from the clerk of the prison A.A. group. I had a faint idea what A.A. was, but that was all. The letter invited me to come to the meetings if I thought I might have a drinking problem. The next Sunday, I attended my first meeting, and when I left that room I had an open mind and an honest desire to stop drinking for the first time in my life.

I have again accepted God as I once knew Him, and once again I ask for His help each morning when I wake up and give Him my thanks each night when I go to bed. I have my loving second wife back again, and she also is an A.A. member now. Last February, I had my first anniversary in A.A. Today, I am living in a minimum-security prison on a farm. I have a parole hearing coming up, and with the grace of God I will be home soon with my wife and family. If it had not been for the spiritual awakening I had that night in my prison cell, if I had not once again come to believe in a Power greater than myself, none of these things I have today would be possible.

Jefferson City, Missouri

A TESTIMONY OF ONE LIFE

What a topsy-turvy life this is! As a pharisee, I used to thank God I was not like the alcoholics I met. I always tried to be a metaphysician-priest; that was my line. (Someone described a metaphysician as one who stumbles into a dark room to look for a black cat that isn't there.) Instead, I became an alcoholic priest.

The progression of this disease catapulted me into outer space. An excess of chemical propellant overworked my sensory mechanism; like the crippled Apollo 13 spacecraft, I was almost stranded on the dark side of the moon. I could not manage the added power; I was not able to control this by myself. I needed a helping Hand, the spiritual reserve of a Higher Power. I felt like a man in a tunnel with no opening at the other end, or like a driver wearing sunglasses at night.

Today, my brain has cleared with the grace of clarity. I am more than clay, more than earth. In the Liturgy of the Eucharist, I daily read that He first blessed this bread, then "He broke it." He tested me with a personal affliction, a recognized disease. The sheath of a seed must be broken to open it to the nurture of the good earth and the warm sun; so I must lose my old self to grow into another, must die in a former life for a renaissance to a new future.

Sometimes I have failed, but I am not a failure; I have made mistakes, but I am not a mistake.

This, then, is a testimony of one life. I must amend crucial chapters of an inner odyssey, never written, never expressed. A vision cleared of fumes and foam can now choose the contents of the next chapter for this human envoy in the service of others. I must give to keep, and never take back.

Now I can dream. After each of us completes his given time here on earth, we will all gather together round the Lord's table in heaven. No one ever returns too late.

Worcester, Massachusetts

AN OPEN HEART

One of those rare moments of insight came to me one Sunday afternoon, as I was trying to read the paper. I was terribly hung-over from a week of round-the-clock drinking. Suddenly, the words on a page hit me: "The number of times that you win or lose is not important. The only thing that matters is the number of times that you try." For several years, I had tried to get someone else to solve my problem for me, but I had not realized I was doing so until that moment of insight. ". . . That *you* try." I was exhilarated. Now I knew that I was an alcoholic and that I had the only qualification for membership in A.A., a desire to stop drinking.

It seemed that I could see a wall crumbling before me—a wall that had separated me from other people. I had never known it existed until I saw it crumbling. Even though I had been considered friendly and gregarious, now I saw that I had really never had a close relationship with anyone. I was not unhappy about this revelation, because, now that my attitude was different, I could remember things people had said at the A.A. meetings I had been attending off and on for three years, and for the first time they had full meaning. Mainly, I remembered and came to understand the words "Keep an open heart."

Prior to this gift of insight, I had not known that my heart was closed. Now I knew—because it was opened. I could now ask and receive help, and I hoped that some day I would have something to give. I felt free and light and good. I would no longer block out love if I kept my heart open.

The next evening, I went to an A.A. meeting with an open heart and a desire to be sober—life's two greatest and most valuable gifts to me. I became a part of that miraculous stream of living known as the Fellowship of A.A. True friends, always available for help, relieve the tensions of my everyday living with myself. They help me, not always with a pat on the back, but sometimes with a warning (like "Take it easy") and always with a sharing attitude (not "You do this," but "I'll do that").

Many spiritual insights have come to me through A.A. since the rare, beautiful moment on a Sunday afternoon, but that was the gift that made it all possible. Each day that I try to have a desire to be sober and to remember to keep an open heart, love and help flow in to me. These bounties are unlimited in A.A. if we are fortunate enough to have the desire. After several years, that moment is still vital—the most vital in my life—and its effect is growing to include non-A.A.'s, as well as A.A.'s, in my world of help.

I had nothing to do with this gift coming to me, so my gratitude is beyond description. It did not take me back to the person I was before drinking or in my active Sunday-school days. It gave me a new life— rather, life itself, because I had attempted suicide and had been hospitalized in private and state mental hospitals. It must have been spiritual; it was neither intellectual nor physical, that's for sure. I believe it was God as I understand Him, working through the love and understanding available in A.A. May I keep my heart open. The joy which can come to an open heart is unlimited.

New York, New York

THE SEARCH 6

You are asking yourself,
as all of us must: "Who am I?" . . .
"Where am I?" . . . "Whence do I go?"
The process of enlightenment is usually
slow. But, in the end, our seeking always
brings a finding. These great mysteries
are, after all, enshrined in
complete simplicity.

Bill W.

Letter, 1955

BREAKTHROUGH

For me, the narrow spiritual path has been one of many and seemingly endless frustrations: three steps forward, two backward, or sometimes four backward. At first, words from the Big Book, from "Alcoholics Anonymous Comes of Age," and from other A.A. literature constantly harassed me. Finally, the pamphlet "Alcoholism the Illness"* forced me to read "The Varieties of Religious Experience," by William James. Bill W. spoke of the immense importance of this book to him. Who was I not to give it at least a look-see? "Just try it for size," an A.A. friend suggested.

As I read the book (skipping over anything I did not understand, which was a great deal on the first reading), it seemed that I was actually beginning to discern my own personal conception of my own personal God. Now at last I saw a real possibility that I might come to know the difference between the spiritual life and the religious life. It was, indeed, this breakthrough that encouraged me to pursue the spiritual beliefs of A.A.

I began talking with people in the program who said they were agnostic. To me, it was interesting and most helpful to become aware of their thinking through private conversation. (Apparently, A.A. agnostics —at any rate, those I talked with—feel that when they speak out, even at closed meetings, their true ideas and sincerity are often misunderstood.) My attendance at spiritual retreats held for alcoholics only also has been of immense value.

Strangely, when I first started this direction of thought, it was inconceivable to me that there was or could be a God personal to me. Now, over five and a half years later, I believe that this God or Higher Power of mine actually and very definitely *loves me*. To Him, I am a complete and total world; He loves me as though I were the only person on earth or anywhere else.

*Now titled "Three Talks to Medical Societies by Bill W."

It no longer is important to my big-shot-ism to go around saying, "I love God"—because I now know myself well enough to realize that I change; I am not constant. It is important for me only to have faith that *God loves me.*

Teaneck, New Jersey

"I'VE GOT IT!"

For about three years in A.A., I had sobriety and that was all. There was something missing, and I knew that it was the spiritual side of the program. I had tried to find it in the Steps and couldn't, perhaps because of my inability to use them as I should have. So I drifted aimlessly along in A.A.—sober, but resentful, negative, and unhappy.

After a glider crash (I was a glider pilot), which injured my back, I suffered from ill health, and my husband decided to take me away on a holiday. When we arrived at a little town on the east coast of South Africa, I was in a very bad mood.

I walked along the beach and along a coral reef. I found a big blowhole where the water was sucked down and then spouted up, and the thought came to me that it would be a very good idea to jump into this hole and finish the life I was leading. I wasn't staying sober for anybody else; I was staying sober for myself. This I knew, and for myself I didn't see any reason to go on living, to stay sober only to reach the state of mind I was in.

While standing there contemplating suicide, I looked out to sea and saw a cloud. This didn't impress me very much, because I knew what a cloud was made of. At the same time, I saw the moon—a day moon, away out at sea—and this didn't impress me very much, either. But then it came to my mind that out there, somewhere, there were stars. I couldn't see them, and yet I knew they were there. This began to have a profound effect on me and my train of thought.

I looked at the waves. I saw them coming in and going out and coming in again. I thought: How useless, how senseless! In and out for millions and millions of years, and all they achieved, it seemed to me, was to break up rocks into tiny pieces and make sea sand. And then I thought of the grain of sand. That grain of sand was made up of atoms; take the atoms away, and there would be no grain of sand. Remove the atoms from the rock I was standing on, and there would be no rock. And I, too, was made up of atoms; remove them, and there would be no me. Remove the atoms from the world, and there would be no world. What held all the atoms together? What held each single atom together?

I realized that the Power holding everything together was my Higher Power. This Power had created me—and I had the audacity to think that I could destroy that which was not mine to destroy.

Within that moment, I changed completely. The thought went through my mind: "You are negative no longer; you are now positive." A great feeling of uplift came over me. With the new joy that filled my heart, I ran down the beach toward my husband, tears pouring down my cheeks, shouting, "I've got it! I've got it!"

He said, "Oh my God, you're drunk again!"

"No!" I said. "The old me just died. You'll never see her again."

And the new one had indeed been born. To this day, he's never seen the old one, nor have I. She died there and then, on those rocks. From that moment onward, I started going from one church to another, seeking, seeking, seeking. One day, somebody said to me, "Stop looking. God has not left. He is here all the time."

There I was, back on the rocky beach, and then I knew that all the time He had been within me.

Port Elizabeth, South Africa

A GLACIER MELTS

I had been sober eighteen months and felt physically and mentally in better health than I had for many years. I was very much involved in A.A. activities, but I remained agnostic about "the Higher Power bit." I considered that I had come to A.A. for sobriety, I had sobriety, and A.A. was all I needed to keep me sober. Occasionally, I wished that I could say, as most A.A. members did, that my Higher Power was God; but the need for honesty had made a strong impression on me, and I knew that I would be unable to admit to a Power higher than Alcoholics Anonymous until I was firmly convinced.

One weekend, I made special, personal plans (setting the stage), and the man included in those plans disappointed me (the actor didn't arrive onstage on cue). Without warning and apparently without any sufficient cause, I was plunged into a fit of hysterical crying and continued to become more emotionally unstrung. I had been hospitalized six years earlier as a psychotic, and now I was experiencing the same feelings of sliding into a pit of hellish torture. I felt as desperate as I had when I made my call for help to A.A. a year and half before. But this time *I was sober.*

My daughter, aged fifteen, became more alarmed than I had ever known her to be in my drinking years. She, too, began to cry from fright, and suggested that I call a doctor or some of my friends in A.A. I said to her, "Linda, no *person* can help me. I need God's help." That word "God" had come out automatically. Previously, I had been unable to say it aloud.

Through tears, my daughter replied, "Mother, I think God has forgotten us." This response caused me to weep even more violently, and I sank into a hopeless depression.

I had attended many, many A.A. meetings, and I had heard the ABC's in Chapter Five of "Alcoholics Anonymous" repeated so often that the answer to my problem was waiting for me in this time of need. I was convinced that God could and would help me if I would seek Him. During the next six weeks, at times when I could be alone, I made a concentrated effort to determine what or who God was and what my relationship was to Him.

Strange things began to happen. I had thought I was happy in that first eighteen months of sobriety, but now everything began to look brighter; people seemed nicer; and I had moments of tremendous insight. It was as if words and sentences I had heard all my life had a deeper meaning and were reaching my feelings, rather than my intellect. It was as if my head and my heart finally had gotten glued together. I no longer seemed like two people in one, engaging in a tug of war. I experienced within this six-week period a feeling of being totally forgiven, and never since have I felt the guilt that I had throughout my life prior to that time. More than once, I had a sense of Presence which I can describe only as being marvelously warm, uplifting, and comforting.

Though I no longer cried while awake during this period, I awakened many times at night because my pillow was wet and cold. It was as if all this weeping were melting a glacier of ice around my heart— a glacier which had cut me off, not only from the world of people, but from the real me. Afterwards, when I confided the strangeness of this time to others in A.A., I was told that I had had "the A.A. cry."

It was a time of confusion, but I was particularly helped by seeing an appendix footnote in the first edition of "Alcoholics Anonymous," acquainting me with the book "The Varieties of Religious Experience," by William James, whose philosophy-psychology is a large part of A.A.'s pragmatic method of gaining sobriety and having a volitional spiritual awakening. As an example, James states (summarizing the views of Dr. E. D. Starbuck), "Now with most of us the sense of our present wrongness is a far more distinct piece of our consciousness than is the imagination of any positive ideal we can aim at. In a majority of cases, indeed, the 'sin' almost exclusively engrosses the attention, so that conversion is *'a process of struggling away from sin rather than of striving towards righteousness.' "* As James describes it, I no longer felt like a divided person. After this period of six weeks, I was unified. Gone from my solar plexus was the "time bomb" that had always been there, waiting to go off.

I believe that I had suffered, not only from alcoholism, but also from "grave emotional and mental disorders." Therefore, it was necessary for me to surrender, not just to alcohol, but to Something Else. No one has said it better than Harry M. Tiebout, M.D., in his pamphlet "The Act of Surrender in the Therapeutic Process": "For a few, there seems to occur a phenomenon of what might be called 'selective surrender.' After the effects of the initial surrender experience have worn away, the individual returns to pretty much the same person he was before, except for the fact that he doesn't drink and has no battle on that line. His surrender is not to life as a person but to alcohol as an alcoholic."

A.A. provided for me a means by which I could overcome the compulsion to drink and, more important, a means by which I could achieve a personality change or spiritual awakening—a surrender to life. Though I have had problems and deep troubles since that summer ten years ago, my faith has not been shaken. I cannot say that I have found God as I understand Him, but rather that I have faith in Something which remains a mystery to me and which I continue to seek.

Fresno, California

THE SEED OF GOD

No one could have been more happy than I, in my early days of A.A. Before that, my fears had become nightmares. If I slept, it was a tortured, restless sleep, and I would awaken to my own cries. Often, I could not sleep at all.

So, when I could once again awaken in the mornings with bright eyes, I felt like a young lad. Now I could laugh again, and I reached the point that I enjoyed this more than alcohol. Each day of sobriety was a testimonial of my attempt to become a human being.

A.A. was right for me—but not the spiritual side of the program. I had already had enough of forced religious training. I was suspicious of the discussions on this subject. A part of a quotation from the Bible, "visiting the iniquity of the fathers upon the children of the third and fourth generation," encompassed me with fear of God's wrath.

But my spiritual growth became stronger from the experiences of others. It was explained to me that I could freely choose a God of my understanding. At first, I thought I was committing a sin by trying to change God, but I soon realized that God was constant, and the only changes that had to be made were in my sick mind. I learned that if you read that Bible quotation in its entirety, God promised "to show mercy to those who love and keep His commandments."

The decision whether to belong to the condemned or to the group enjoying mercy and compassion was mine. At that time, I didn't have the requirements for recovery. Instead of complete surrender, I set up forced rules for myself. I failed to ask God for help and guidance and tried to follow these self-imposed rules instead. But when I failed, I did ask God's forgiveness, and I promised to do better. My A.A. sponsor advised me that, to get help from our Higher Power, we ourselves must ask—in humility and sincerity. Another person, however good and wise, cannot plant the seed of God within us. God alone can do this. My problem was to find this sprout among the weeds in my mind. Is it not true that there is some good in each of us?

To me, God's creations are works of perfection. Even *I* am a miracle, developed from a tiny seed, which had concealed within it all of my own future qualities and even those of generations yet to come. A scientist is but a common laborer compared to the Higher Power. Science bases its knowledge on hypotheses; compared to God's wisdom, man's has only remotely touched the truth.

Still, I can believe in the scientific theories that all activity is electronic motion, and so it is very easy to imagine that we are governed by an even greater electronic force. God is alive, and the universe revolves around Him, even as the electrons do around the core of an atom. I cannot comprehend what is inside a tiny electron, any more than I can visualize what is beyond outer space. I know not how a cell is born, nor where I go in eternity. Scientists have said that the cells of the body are renewed every eight years. If this is true, then my body and I are separate entities, since I have survived the whole metamorphosis of my body over and over.

The world, too, is changing constantly, and I am no longer afraid of this change. I want to be a part of it and its new developments. I have been shown, and fully believe today, that faith can move mountains. I once encountered many blind alleys, but today, as long as I have faith, my path is clear.

This has all been slow progress for me. Like so many, I do not always surrender completely; I allow the cares and worries of the day to distort my thinking. But as soon as I get back on the right track, I realize that I have everything I need.

Whatever problems confront me, large or small, they can be solved wisely. Or they can be solved my way. The choice is mine. If I want to know God's will, I must pause and ask, "What would God have me do?" Why, then, is it so difficult for me just to pause, to meditate, and to allow God to guide me? The reason is my ego. I know—though sometimes I forget—that by myself my capabilities are nil. I could not, now or ever, develop the most minute electron.

When my days were filled with fears and I was trying desperately to hang on, I discovered that I could take the Third Step and be on firm ground. I have since taken this Step countless times. I actually experience a sense of physical freedom when I give up to the demands of life. "To leave all and follow Thee" means for me total acceptance, even of that which I would not desire for myself—such as misfortune, poverty, illness, and even death. I completely surrender my life and my thinking to my Higher Power. After all, when the world comes to an end some day, it will do so without my permission.

Helsinki, Finland

TO THE FOURTH STEP

Even at an early age, booze was no stranger to me. I remember crawling from one soused parent to another for a mouthful of beer. As I grew older, the craving for the stuff drove me to find more. Too young to get a good job, I turned to thievery. I was a good thief—I thought. The law soon deflated that balloon.

On my second trip to jail, I attended my first A.A. meeting, with strong recommendations from the authorities. All the members greeted me and talked about how the Twelve Steps had helped them and, in turn, should help me. For some mysterious reason, the conversation turned toward God, religion, and an unidentifiable "Higher Power." Oh-oh! I didn't want anything to do with something even remotely connected with religion. "Besides," I said, "I'm not an alcoholic." I had just turned nineteen.

Although I kept attending meetings, I couldn't accept the religious aspect. After I got out, booze went on flowing down my gullet until one morning I awoke in the strangest place—at home! That did it. That very night, my mother and I both attended an A.A. meeting.

Sobriety was a novelty, and for fourteen years I enjoyed it. The humble business I started grew and prospered. I had become part of the human race. It was great!

Then business pressure began to mount, and I suddenly couldn't face those simple problems. That was when my old enemy reappeared. I couldn't resist that one little drink, for old times' sake. Business profits took a plunge; alcohol gained steadily; once again, I found myself in court.

I was horrified when the judge said, "You are charged with the theft of sixty-four bottles of whiskey. I have no alternative but to sentence you to a Federal penitentiary."

"You can't send me to a penitentiary!" I roared. "I haven't got the time!"

The spectators laughed aloud until the gavel fell. I hung my head low in the realization that they were laughing at me. I don't know how long after that embarrassing day it was before I remembered the Twelve Steps and made the Fourth Step work for me. I asked myself questions and answered them truthfully. This done, I joined the prison A.A. group.

For me, that inventory is a higher power, God, and willpower all combined into one. Step Four was all I needed. This time, there was no mention of religion, much to my relief. We discussed the force, power, or object that for each one of us had been our higher power. You see, anything connected in any way with religion is frowned on, to say the least, by us. Yet I have seen many members of this group leave and never return to booze or prison.

Agnostic, you say? Certainly. But that, too, has been an advantage for me. My search for a God that I could not find led me to Step Four. This Step, I feel confident, will help me stay sober.

Waupun, Wisconsin

BACK TO THE FUNDAMENTALS

A.A. was asking me, of all people, to believe in God. Not only that, they were asking me to believe so thoroughly that I'd be willing to turn my life and my will over to God as I understood Him.

I didn't understand him. I didn't know anything about Him. In one way or another, I had been a Catholic, a Baptist, a Presbyterian, an Episcopalian, a Lutheran, and a Christian Scientist, and I'd even been exposed to some extent to the beliefs of Mormons, Mennonites, and Quakers. When I was in college, I specialized in ancient history and got very interested in the mystics. Also, I learned something about Muhammadanism, Buddhism, the mythology of the Vikings, the Romans, and the ancient Greeks, and the original, primitive, pagan religions. But I still couldn't believe.

I tried reading the Bible, but I bogged down so hopelessly in the terminology that it was pathetic. So I turned to small books written by Bible scholars. "Maybe I'm learning something," I thought, "or maybe

I'm just getting confused. But I've got to keep on with this, because at least I'm staying sober."

I was still going to A.A. meetings and talking to older members who had been sober for a long time. Many of them had a smile in their eyes while we talked—they had already been through this. One of them advised me to go back to the Bible, especially to the Sermon on the Mount, the condensation of Jesus' message. After we had discussed it, I was able to take from this reading three things that helped me—that I could relate to my A.A. life.

Love your neighbor. Where else but in A.A. could you find half a million people dedicated to love, and really loving each other? The love of one alcoholic for another is something never seen before in the history of the world.

Do unto others as you would have them do unto you. In A.A., we do unto others what's already been done unto us. We help others as we have been helped.

As you think, so shall you be. I grew to believe that every deed we perform in our entire lives is just the outward manifestation of an inward thought. If there was a glass of whiskey in front of me, my hand couldn't reach out and pick it up. My hand and arm are not capable of independent action. The only thing that could make my hand reach out and take that glass and bring it up to my lips would be a thought in my head: "Hand, reach out and take the glass."

While I was making some progress, I still didn't have a concept of God. So I went back to the Big Book, as I had done so many times before with other problems. The answer I was looking for was on page 12, in Ebby's words to Bill: " *'Why don't you choose your own conception of God?'* "

"I've tried everything else," I thought, "and I've got no place else to go. I might just as well." I sat down at my desk, got a pad of paper and a pencil, and asked myself, "If you could pick the kind of God that you *could* believe in, what would He be like?" I bore in mind the facts that I was an alcoholic and that I had been a perfectionist all my life. The world was never perfect enough for me. Everything that I ever believed in, every ideal that I ever followed turned out to have feet of clay. Here was my chance. For the first time in my life, I could create something perfect. All right!

I wrote across the page, "God is the perfection I've been searching for all my life. He is too perfect to have human characteristics and faults." That was the start.

Then I wrote, "God is the ultimate perfection. He is the perfect love, the perfect truth, the perfect goodness, the perfect understanding, tolerance, mercy, forgiveness. God is so perfect that no matter how evil, how unclean we may be, He'll forgive us if we ask, and grant us strength to overcome our shortcomings."

I sat back and told myself, "You're a brain! You've come up with something brand-new here." And then I realized that I was no big brain —just a dunce. This was the God that Jesus was talking about two thousand years ago, when He stood on the hillside and said He had a Father in heaven who loved all human beings. Then I thought, "What is the one theme that will pull all this together in my mind?" I had a strange feeling that I was getting close.

At one time, the great jurist Oliver Wendell Holmes was asked what his religion was. And he answered that his whole concept of God could be found in the first two words of the Lord's Prayer.

So I got out a copy of the Lord's Prayer and looked at it. The first word was "Our." It didn't say "your," "my," "her," or "his." It said, "Our Father . . ." He is the Father to all of us. He created every one of us.

I happen to be a father myself—one of the world's worst, but no matter how sick or how bad I got in my days of drinking, I never once wished any harm to my own children. Nothing but the best for them! And I have to assume that this is what our Father wishes for us. He created us, and He cares what happens to us. He didn't create me to die a drunk in an alley.

We're not just some higher form of animal that's got a little better brain and a thumb that can meet the first finger to grasp a weapon or light a fire and so make us superior. We're a different breed entirely. We're unique because of the universal law that like begets like—a rosebush can't produce a lily of the valley, and a cow can't produce a colt. If God is a spiritual being, then we are spiritual beings.

Warren, Pennsylvania

THIS SPIRIT TOUCH

After nine months of Alcoholics Anonymous and a few slips, I had a terrible bout with resentment, self-pity, and two bottles. The next morning—a beautiful, fresh spring morning—an alcoholic awakening came: "This I never have to do again!" I was free, ready to learn what A.A. was all about—the marvelous way of life, so simple in structure, so profound in practice. We must never let a newcomer know before he is ready how God springs His magnificent trap and teaches us that love means responding.

Four years later, vicissitudes came close together in our family—a disappointment, a long terminal illness, and three deaths. During those sad times, friends lent my husband and me their apartment at a southern beach. It was in this quiet interlude that a "moment electric" occurred in my life—a God-given new awareness. The wings of the spirit were unfurled, and ever since I have been learning to use these wings.

I have learned that others grow these wings more slowly, without a "moment electric," and that theirs still are strong and beautiful. I have also learned that others have been given this experience and then have thrown their wings away, because they mistakenly thought that the Absolute would sustain them automatically. I weep for them, because they did not gather that half the beauty of a gift lies in the manner in which it is received. They did not respond.

At some time, perhaps in a more moderate way, nearly everyone has experienced this spirit touch of God—the fleeting feeling of insight, love, joy, and "The world is right." Once, I thought that only unusual circumstances made these moments possible. Actually, I now think, they are forecasts of what one can have if one is willing to take the time and make the effort. Peace, love, and joy can be sought through quiet thinking and honest prayer. The wholeness, the new awareness, that is produced affects one's relationship with God and man to a degree greater than would seem possible in ordinary life. The clamor of now is reduced; understanding is increased. Feelings become something to explore, rather than to suppress. These moments are not ends in themselves, but strengthening links in a chain of events. A deepness within is opened— calm, restful, glorious depths. There is a joining of inner forces with outer forces. The Power greater than ourselves puts us in tune with the world. Of course, there are times when the instrument is out of key, and then we have an insatiable desire to find the key again.

Undoubtedly, this way of life is different for each person, because each becomes his true self in relation to others, as well as to himself. Everything becomes filled with purpose, whether it is small or large, ugly or beautiful. In the life of the spirit, there is no small, there is no ugly. Paradoxically, inwardness increases the importance of other people and of one's surroundings. All five senses are more alert. The feeling is one of completeness.

Sometimes, I am at ease in the world for days at a time. Then this serenity goes away, but the understanding continues. My shortcomings have not disappeared—anger, self-pity, hastiness, envy, selfishness, resentments. But they have lessened, because now I know that when I do not exert control over these shortcomings, the harmony of completeness vanishes.

My talents have not improved particularly, but I take more enjoyment in those I possess, through immersion in each moment of doing. My relationships with others are more involving, especially in the one-to-one encounter.

There is a marvelous sense of timing during these days of completeness. A watch isn't necessary; each action dovetails with the next. No one moment seems more important than another; each moment is full. This, perhaps, is real prayer. *I* have nothing to do with the joyance that comes forth; it is as though I spoke with other tongues. How this happens is a mystery, but it is remarkable to see the surprised reactions of others and to know that their lives, too, may be changed for a moment.

I believe completeness is waiting for anyone who will take the time to make the effort, through quiet thinking, honest prayer, chosen reading, and exercise. These are the ingredients. It is an adventure so worthwhile that all else fades in comparison, yet it makes all else worthwhile.

Richmond, Virginia

COINCIDENCE?

*Faith in a Power
greater than ourselves,
and miraculous demonstrations
of that Power in human
lives are facts as old
as man himself.*

Bill W.

"Alcoholics Anonymous," page 55

WHY? I DON'T KNOW

When I came to A.A., I no longer believed in the God of my youth, a personal God who would help me as an individual. After being in A.A. quite awhile, I tried to take the Twelve Steps to the best of my ability, in the order in which they were written. It was a slow and painful path, but I did not give up; I kept on trying.

Step Three, I now believe, was the key that opened some door within my being and allowed spirituality to enter, not in a sudden flow, but as a trickle, on occasions just a drop at a time. As I progressed through the Steps, I began to see some change in my thinking and my attitudes toward people. At the completion of Step Nine, I now believe, I did have a spiritual awakening. I came to the point where, not only could I give love and compassion to my fellowman, but, more important, I could receive love and compassion. Now spiritual experiences, as I understand them, began to happen.

At a recent A.A. state convention, Bill came up and introduced himself and said that he had heard me talk at an area meeting in a small town in Tennessee, more than three years earlier. That was Bill's first A.A. meeting. After hearing my story, he decided to do something about his drinking problem and became a member of A.A. Bill has not had a drink since that Sunday afternoon when he attended his first meeting. What did I say? I don't remember. Why was it necessary for me to be 300 miles from my home on a summer Sunday afternoon in order for Bill to get the message of A.A.? I don't know. . . .

One Saturday morning, I decided to go see Ken. I had known him casually for twenty-five years, and I knew that he had a serious drinking problem; but I hadn't seen or spoken to him for a number of years. I knocked on his front door and asked him whether he remembered me. He said, "Yes," and invited me in. I asked him how he was doing, and he said, "Fine." I asked him how he was getting along with his drinking problem, and he said, "Oh, not too much trouble."

I told him part of my story. As I stood up to leave, I said, "How about going to a meeting with me tonight?" He said he would, and I told him I would pick him up. But when I returned that evening, Ken had decided not to go. I said, "Okay. I'll pick you up Monday night at the same time." Monday night, he was asleep, and his son said he didn't want to go to the meeting. Tuesday, after work, I called Ken to say that I would stop by and take him to a meeting. When I arrived at his home, he was sitting on the front porch waiting for me. As we were about to enter the meeting room, Ken saw through the doorway a man that he had drunk with for a number of years. This man had been sober for eighteen months. Ken now makes three to four meetings a week, has not had a drink since his first A.A. meeting, and in a short time will get his first-year chip.

Why did I decide that Saturday morning to go to see Ken, who had never called A.A.? I don't know. Why did Ken refuse to go to the first two meetings and then agree to go to the third, where he would meet his old friend and so have an immediate relationship with a recovering alcoholic? I don't know. . . .

I don't attempt to explain with reason and logic why these things happen. When they happen, I just accept them. I feel perhaps that God, as I understand Him, found it necessary for me to suffer the pain and anguish of an addicted alcoholic and to go through the slow and, for me, difficult program of recovery in A.A. in order to be prepared and willing to do His will. I am grateful and thankful that God has given this to me. Perhaps it is because I take the Third Step every morning. My hopes and prayers are that each day I will be able to maintain this conscious contact with God.

Kingsport, Tennessee

A RAINY NIGHT

After I had been sober some four years, there was a culmination of problems I couldn't face. I retreated from these problems without the aid of the bottle, but the reaction from this experience was severe—what many of us call a dry drunk. It was very frightening; I was motivated by all kinds of fears, and I couldn't distinguish reality from hallucinations.

I was living in a room in a seaside resort, out of season, while I tried different ways to straighten out my thinking. Little chores like washing my socks and shorts would take an hour. It would take an endless amount of time to dress; many times, I didn't know whether I was dressing or undressing. I would stop, sit down, and try to pray; but I couldn't get past "Our Father" in the Lord's Prayer. Then I would leave the room and walk ten or fifteen miles, trying to become exhausted enough to sleep.

This had been going on for about a month, and during this period my family left me. My health was waning; I had gone from 170 pounds down to 118 pounds, and I was getting desperate. There seemed to be all sorts of plots against me. If I passed people on the street talking, I imagined they were plotting against me. I also imagined someone was putting hallucinogens into my food. I wasn't able to sleep at all.

In the seaside resort, I visited an attorney's office to collect some money I had coming to me. As he had known me when I was normal, he tried to help me by sending me to the library to look something up for him. He thought this might help me forget my troubles. I walked into the library, and (due to the death, I suppose, of one of the town fathers) the walls were all draped in black. In my mixed-up mind, I thought that the mourning was for me and that it was some kind of directive. In other words, I had come to the end of my time.

At six p.m., the library closed and I had to leave. It was a cold and rainy night in March, yet I started up the boardwalk for my nightly walk. I believed that the seeming directive had told me to walk into the ocean. There was a deserted pier about a mile down the boardwalk, and I planned to walk out on this and step off. Full of fears, I walked along, worrying that I wouldn't have the courage to fulfill the directive and asking the Higher Power for strength and help to do what I thought was required of me.

Only a block or so from the pier, I saw a man approaching from the opposite direction, with his head down, walking into the rain. When he came to me, he stopped and smiled, and I recognized him as a priest I knew from home. I told him I was very ill. He then sat on a bench with me in the rain and assured me that in time all my troubles would pass and the day would come when I would understand them. He said I was not to do anything foolish, but ask God's help, and somehow everything would work out.

The feeling that I had to destroy myself vanished. Although I remained quite ill for several months more, the thought of self-destruction never again entered my mind.

Quite some time passed. Once again, I was well and an active member of A.A. One night, I attended a meeting—and there was that same priest, as a guest speaker. I decided to ask him whether he remembered meeting me that March night, while walking in the rain. By this time, I was convinced that it had been a hallucination. But he told me he did remember and was very happy that I was well and back on the beam. He explained that he had gone to the seaside resort to address a convention of educators. He was sick of sitting in the hotel room; so, rain or not, he went out for some air. I believe now that the One taking care of me must have given him a little push.

Since then, almost thirteen years ago, I have been a successful member of the program.

Spring Lake Heights, New Jersey

GOD WAS THE POSTMAN

It began on a somber October day, when I awoke with memories of Pat, my second wife. As I reflected, soberly, on our twenty months of marriage, I remembered her charismatic ways, her striking mind, her quiet charm, and her repeated, futile attempts to stay sober in A.A., where we had met. I had been sober for three years then. But I suppose that I had not truly experienced a spiritual awakening in A.A. For that basic reason, most likely, I returned to drinking after Pat died, and I plunged to a terrifying new bottom. There's always a new bottom, you know.

On that October morning, the second anniversary of her death, I was in my third week of renewed sobriety. I became more depressed as I recalled our life together, and I bolted to an A.A. meeting, where I described my returning grief and loneliness. There, I was given understanding and compassion that lifted my lagging spirits.

For almost a year, absorbed in my alcoholic oblivion and shame, I had not written to my two teen-aged children. I refused, in my irrational thinking, to admit that they could be aware I was drinking again. But now I had written to them twice—letters I had been capable of writing solely because of rejoining A.A. I had asked the kids to forgive me, bared my drinking, admitted my self-engulfed negligence toward them, and prayed they would somehow respond. For days, I had kept my eyes on the mailbox with anguish and fear—fear that neither of my children would reply.

On that October day, the mailman arrived with a letter from my fifteen-year-old son, who had had to undergo psychiatric treatment after his mother left me. His words are particularly thrilling when you realize that he hasn't been exposed to Alateen, but, rather, to the bitterness my first wife, his mother, still feels about me. His letter reads:

"I received your second letter today. I got your first letter a week ago, but I didn't get down to writing you till today. I'm very sorry.

"I love you very much. You don't know how glad I was to hear from you.

"I don't believe in condemning people. I have never condemned you, and the day I do will be the day I die. Condemnation is for people who are so small that they put other people down to make themselves feel big.

"I love you and I forgive you. I'd be a liar to say I wasn't disappointed. But that's all in the past. The past is gone. It's dead. We can't relive it or bring it back.

"I know how you must feel—guilty and ashamed. Don't worry. I'm on your side. You can count on me to try to understand and help you."

As I read the letter, I cried, softly and gratefully. Yes, Pat was dead; but her death was, like my drinking, a matter of yesterday.

My son's simple, love-infused letter had not reached me on that heart-trying day through coincidence. God was the postman. He made sure I would receive this inspiration, which in turn became my concept of His revelation. And He delivers each day (if I look for it) a fresh message of love, forgiveness, mercy, hope, and opportunity—the message that thousands, like Pat, cannot or will not see.

Southgate, Michigan

MATHEMATICAL MIRACLE

Some years ago, I heard a story which has been making the rounds in Midwest A.A. circles for years. I don't have any names to back up this story, but I have heard it from many sources, and the circumstances sound believable. . . .

A man in a small Wisconsin city had been on the program for about three years and had enjoyed contented sobriety through that period. Then bad luck began to hit him in bunches. The firm for which he had worked for some fifteen years was sold; his particular job was phased out of existence, and the plant moved to another city. For several months, he struggled along at odd jobs while looking for a company that needed his specialized experience. Then another blow hit him. His wife was forced to enter a hospital for major surgery, and his company insurance had expired.

At this point he cracked, and decided to go on an all-out binge. He didn't want to stage this in the small city, where everyone knew his sobriety record. So he went to Chicago, checked in at a North Side hotel, and set forth on his project. It was Friday night, and the bars were filled with a swinging crowd. But he was in no mood for swinging—he just wanted to get quietly, miserably drunk.

Finally, he found a basement bar on a quiet side street, practically deserted. He sat down on a bar stool and ordered a double bourbon on the rocks. The bartender said, "Yes, sir," and reached for a bottle.

Then the bartender stopped in his tracks, took a long, hard look at the customer, leaned over the bar, and said in a low tone, "I was in Milwaukee about four months ago, and one night I attended an open meeting. You were on the speaking platform, and you gave one of the finest A.A. talks I ever heard." The bartender turned and walked to the end of the bar.

For a few minutes, the customer sat there—probably in a state of shock. Then he picked his money off the bar with trembling hands and walked out, all desire for a drink drained out of him.

It is estimated that there are about 8,000 saloons in Chicago, employing some 25,000 bartenders. This man had entered the one saloon in 8,000 where he would encounter the one man in 25,000 who knew that he was a member of A.A. and didn't belong there.

Chicago, Illinois

SOMETHING WAS WRONG

Let me stress straightaway that, although I come of a family with strong religious beliefs and attended church in my youth, I had no idea what it was all about and wasn't really concerned. I attended church merely to keep my parents off my back. When, as a teen-ager, I began to drift away from my parents, I also began to drift away from church, and I don't recall ever again going on my knees to pray—until I was introduced to Alcoholics Anonymous in a mental hospital in Glasgow, after eighteen years of sick drinking.

In this hospital, I begged God for help; my tormented mind would not allow me to pray for it. Each day, I asked God to ease this endless torment, only to awake each morning with the same pressure and endless despair. But I kept on asking God for help, and slowly my mind began to unwind. I realized that something wonderful was happening to me. As a person with little or no faith, I wasn't sure whether I was being helped by the hospital treatment, the A.A. meetings in the hospital, or God. So I clung tight to all three.

As time favored me, I began to realize that a Power much greater than anything I had known was helping to restore me to sanity. I put myself in the hands of this great Power, now known to me as God.

Shortly after this, I was released from the hospital, and I was at home when I experienced a very close but frightening conscious contact with the divine Power. It all started one Sunday afternoon, as I was sitting reading the newspapers. For no apparent reason, I got a very strange feeling that something was wrong with an A.A. friend who was in hospital after a slip.

I went to the hospital right away—and found my friend crying his heart out. He had just received the news that his brother had died, two hours earlier.

On leaving the hospital, after consoling my friend, I was walking down the road when I was suddenly filled by a very moving and frightening power, which seemed to take me over completely. I stopped and looked up into the night sky. I felt that I was up in a cloud, and God was inside me. I couldn't sleep at all that night; I was in very deep thought. The next day, I felt completely at peace with the world.

After a time, although I still maintained peace of mind, I began to experience a feeling of emptiness which I could not understand. It wasn't until I tried to be completely honest with myself and to practice the A.A. principles in all my affairs that this emptiness was replaced by joy.

It is my belief that the feeling of emptiness was my own doing. I had been so elated by that wonderful experience on the road at night that I wanted to stay up in a cloud with God. But this was not to be. It was my place to be down among the suffering alcoholics, not up in a cloud. As long as I keep my feet on the ground, among the suffering, God will come down and remain always with me.

It is not my intention to reform anyone or to pretend to be a Holy Joe. I am just a grateful soul who hopes to help someone find peace and happiness and then share it with someone else.

Glasgow, Scotland

A
HIGHER
POWER

*Our concepts
of a Higher Power and
God—as we understand Him—
afford everyone a nearly
unlimited choice of spiritual
belief and action.*

Bill W.

A.A. Grapevine, April 1961

MY FRIEND

I have recently made a friend of Someone I wish everyone could know. This Friend is never too busy to listen to me, my problems, my joys, and my sorrows. He gives me the courage to face life squarely and helps me conquer my fears. The counsel I get is always good, for this Friend is wise, patient, and tolerant. Sometimes, I do not heed His advice, and then I must ask for and be willing to accept additional advice very humbly and sincerely.

Regardless of the mistakes I make, my Friend is always there, available to me at any time, day or night. I can talk, and He does not interrupt, no matter how I ramble on. Sometimes, while talking to Him, I receive a solution to my problem. Other times, just by putting my problem into words, I see how petty and unimportant it is. I feel as if my Friend is holding my hand and gently guiding me if I will listen. I feel that when I do not listen, my Friend is hurt, but never angry.

My Friend is with me at work or at home, my constant companion wherever I go. He is my Higher Power as I understand it. He is the God I know.

Colorado Springs, Colorado

AN ATHEIST'S JOURNEY

Four members of an A.A. group were called by a hospital as a last resort, a token gesture, to see a man who was in a nearly hopeless mental and physical state. He was due to be committed to a state institution as an incurable alcoholic, and almost certainly that would be his final home. A.A.? Well, he decided, nothing could be worse than what he was facing. So he agreed to listen, on one condition: He didn't want "any of that God stuff." He was a professed atheist, and on that one point he was clear; he had no intention of changing, no matter what the consequences.

The four men talked; he listened; and when they had finished, he was interested. There was still the big drawback, however—God. If that idea was part of the program, A.A. was not for him. The four men thought, and then suddenly one of them spoke, quietly at first, unsure of how his new approach would be received. He pointed out the plight of the patient, his helplessness, his illness. As he talked, he became more certain he was taking the right path. He pointed out that he and the other three were sober and had managed to stay that way. They were working; they were happy. Surely, this made them stronger than the patient. The patient couldn't argue that point. Well then, couldn't they be considered a higher power of a sort, who possibly could help restore his sanity?

He thought about this, and somewhere deep in the shadowy, confused recesses of his mind, there flashed a faint hope. Yes, he told them, they could represent his higher power; he could turn his life over to their care. The four men looked at one another. At least, it was a place to start, but it wouldn't be easy.

It was indeed a long, slow process, but gradually the cobwebs began to clear. As the patient read more and more about A.A., he eagerly looked forward to the visits from his first four friends and from the other members of the group who were now coming to see him, too. His body took much longer to heal than his mind, so it was a red-letter day when he was finally able to dress and say goodbye to the hospital and to all the doctors and nurses who had helped restore him to physical health. As he dressed, he kept thinking how different this was from the departure he had almost made, to the state institution. His trust, his belief in four men had made it possible. But could he stay sober outside these doors? Well, he'd do it *today*, anyhow.

He threw himself into A.A. work with all the energy he could muster, attending several meetings a week. His body still tired quickly, but he was never too tired to answer a Twelfth Step call. The memory of his first visit from A.A. and what it had meant to him would always be clear.

One day, a call came for him to see someone who needed help. When he arrived, he discovered that fate had indeed dealt him a strange hand. The alcoholic he was visiting was a priest. He played that hand carefully and wisely, for it was a challenge unlike any he had ever faced or had ever imagined facing. He, who had shunned this man's God, must now find exactly the right words for communication. He fumbled for a start, and then suddenly it became easy to talk to this priest—this fellow alcoholic. A warm friendship developed between the two, and so it was a special joy when he became the priest's sponsor. They learned much from each other. Or perhaps, in each case, the knowledge had been there all along, just waiting for the right person to bring it to the surface.

In his remaining years, this man was called upon many more times to help someone find the way to sobriety. Of these calls, two took him to the side of other men of the cloth who needed help—in these cases, ministers. Twice more, he was privileged to sponsor men of God—by now his God, as well.

He left this world after seven years of uninterrupted sobriety, a man at peace with himself and his Higher Power. His legacy is the same as that left by A.A.'s everywhere, the world over, more valuable than any earthly riches. It is a living legacy, embodied in the men and women he has helped and in the alcoholics to whom they, in turn, have extended a hand.

Sioux City, Iowa

THE ONLY REALITY

I'm so tired of wandering around in my dreams, yet my "I" keeps driving me back to them. For me, the only way out of it is through God. He is the only reality there is, and everything else must start from Him.

A.A. Internationalists

REASON OR CONSCIENCE?

When I first heard the advice "Listen to God," I looked around to see who was present. People who listened to voices were, I supposed, kept in some place at the expense of the state. Since I was already in one of those places, I figured that if I tried listening and someone in authority was watching me, I would not have a snowball's hope in the Other Place of ever getting out.

Then one day I did try listening to God, and found that He had been talking to me for some time. About those checks I had cashed, knowing that they would bounce. About those rotten lies I had told. About some relationships I would not have wanted made into a movie. About the selfishness of my ways and the grievous hurt I had inflicted on my friends and relatives.

That's right. God talked to me through my conscience. Of course, when I was knocking off the hooch in a manner calculated to create an acute shortage of the stuff, a Higher Power just did not exist for me, and the old conscience had a very thin time. When I came to believe, my conscience reasserted itself, and now (egged on by my conscience) I am endeavoring to make amends for all my wrongdoings in the past, as Step Nine suggests.

Reason (or common sense, if you prefer) is another method of finding out the will of God, but I prefer to rely on my conscience. During my drinking days, my reason told me that I was jeopardizing my health, my job, my bank balance, and a host of other things. Where did this ordinary human reasoning get me? It got me two slips of paper: one from my boss, saying that he thought he could manage without my services; the other from my bank manager, reminding me that, although he had lots of money, he thought I had had more than my fair share of it. My "reason" brought me to a mental and physical breakdown, which led me to that spell in an institution. Human wisdom had failed; I needed a wisdom greater—far greater—than my own. This I found when I found a Higher Power in my conscience.

All I have to do now is assemble all the facts as I see them, and let Him mold them to a conclusion. The conclusion at which I arrive is that God's power is shown through results. How many times have we followed a course of action on faith alone, and then told ourselves, when results verified the rightness of our action, that we must be psychic. Psychic? Nonsense! Have you ever been of two (or more) minds when trying to arrive at a decision, and then suddenly found something quite circumstantial popping up to show you the way? I have, and to me this is just one more item to be added to the long list of God's accomplishments for me—guidance.

I do not have to be guided to shave each morning, nor to have a bath (however occasionally), nor can I rely on supernatural intervention to help me slosh a golf ball the way it ought to be sloshed. But I have been guided to know that I must make amends for the grief and worry I visited on my loved ones during the dark days. When, in all humility, I try to pass our message on to other less fortunate alcoholics, I know that the plan of the Higher Power comes to us through the medium of people. To us alcoholics, this does not mean common or garden people, but special people, such as other alcoholics. And I am guided to include among the people from whom I might receive guidance, and to whom I must demonstrate the life of my conscience or Higher Power, those who married me, loved me, befriended me, and stuck by me, as others stuck by other alcoholics.

It matters not whether reason or conscience showed me the way. I came to believe in a Power greater than myself, and that has been my salvation.

Bulawayo, Rhodesia

INNER VOICE

Long before nagging and pressures from others concerning my excessive use of alcohol made any impression on me, the nagging voice of conscience—my own inner voice of truth and right—apprised me of the irrevocable fact that I had lost control of alcohol, that I was powerless. I know now that the inner voice was God, as I understand Him, speaking. For, as I had been taught from earliest memory and as A.A. has emphasized, God—or good—emanates from within each of us.

Lakewood, Ohio

FAITH IN PEOPLE

My parents gave me a faith that in later years I lost. No, it was not a religious faith, though I was exposed to the teachings of two sects. Neither was forced upon me; I simply drifted away through boredom, and my fragile, superficial belief in God vanished as soon as I tried thinking about it.

It was a faith in people that my parents gave me—both by loving me and by respecting me as an individual, entitled to make my own choices. This love I accepted and returned unquestioningly, as a fact of nature.

Out in the world on my own, I still had a feeling of being under benevolent protection; my immediate bosses (of both sexes) seemed to regard me as kindly as schoolteachers had. Oddly, my good fortune sometimes annoyed me. "What is this?" I asked myself. "Do I arouse the maternal impulse?" For there was inside me an element at war with my faith in people. It was a furious, stiff-necked pride, an urge for total independence. With my contemporaries, I was always painfully shy, and even then I interpreted this handicap correctly as a symptom of egotism —a fear that others would not agree with my own high valuation of myself.

That valuation certainly did not include a picture of myself as a drunk. Often, I suspect that pride kills as many alcoholics as liquor does. I could very easily have been one of the victims, because my reaction to fast-progressing alcoholism was chiefly a frantic effort to hide it. Ask for help? What an idea!

The day came when my pride was squashed flat (temporarily), and I did call for help. I called on people—strangers. But my pride, expanding as health returned, blocked my first two approaches to A.A.

(During this interlude, nonalcoholic friends helped me, too—unasked.) After one more failure to regain my skill as a social drinker, I was convinced, and I began my A.A. membership in earnest.

Fortunately, I joined a group that devotes its closed meetings to Step discussions. Most of the members had their own concepts of a personal God; the atmosphere of faith surrounding me was so marked that I thought at times I was on the point of joining in it. I never did. And yet I found the Steps revealing new depths of meaning with each discussion.

In Step Two, the "Power greater than ourselves" meant A.A., but not just the members I knew. It meant all of us, everywhere, sharing a concern for each other and thereby creating a spiritual resource stronger than any one of us could provide. Another woman in my group believed that the souls of dead alcoholics, including those of times before A.A., contributed to this fountainhead of goodwill. The thought was so beautiful that I wished I could believe it, too.

At first, Step Three was simply the way I felt on no-hangover mornings of early sobriety, sitting by my window on days that always seemed sunny, having no immediate prospect of employment, and feeling perfectly happy and confident anyhow. Then the Step became a cheerful acceptance of my place in the world: "I have no idea Who or What is running the show, but I know *I'm* not!" And I could also see Step Three as a good attitude, an effective approach to life: "If I am swimming in salt water and I panic and start thrashing around and fighting it, it will drown me. But if I relax and have faith in it, it will hold me afloat."

Though Step Four does not mention a Higher Power, to me the word "moral" carried an implication of sin, which in my book translates as an offense against God. So I regarded the inventory instead as an attempt at an honest description of my character; on the red side went qualities that tended to hurt people. By trying to live in the world, rather than escape from it, by trying to open myself up to other people, rather than withdraw from them, I hoped that this contact with my fellow human beings would somehow rub off the sharp, hurtful corners of my personality—Steps Six and Seven.

I am not sure that I was consciously working the Steps, but they were surely working on me. In about the fourth year of sobriety, a trivial incident suddenly made me realize that my old bugaboo of shyness had disappeared. "I feel at home in the world!" I said to myself in astonishment.

Now, some ten years later, I still do. In the whole measure of my life, the benefits of the A.A. experience have far outweighed the damages of active alcoholism. What was it that overcame my pride (for the moment) and made me reachable? The best answer I can find is what my father used to call "the life force." (He was an old-fashioned family doctor, and he had seen that force springing up or failing many times.) It is in all of us, I believe; it animates all living things; it keeps the galaxies wheeling. The salt-water metaphor applied to Step Three was not chosen by accident, for to me the ocean is a symbol of this force; I come closest to Step Eleven when I can contemplate an unbroken horizon from the deck of a ship. I am cut down to size; I feel serenely that I am a small part of something vast and unknowable.

But isn't the ocean rather a cold symbol? Yes. Do I think that its eye is on the minnow, that it is concerned about any individual's fate? Would I talk to it? No. Once, near the end of my drinking, I did address three words to Something nonhuman. In the darkness before morning, I got out of bed, knelt, folded my hands, and said, "Please help me." Then I shrugged and said, "Who'm I talking to?" and got back into bed.

When I related that incident to one of my sponsors, she said, "But He *did* answer your prayer."

That may be. But I do not feel it. I didn't argue with her, nor do I attack the mystery with pure logic now. If you could prove to me logically that there is a personal God—and I don't think you can—I still would not be inclined to talk to a Presence I couldn't *feel*. If I could prove to you logically that there is no God—and I know I can't—your true faith would not be shaken. In other words, matters of faith lie entirely outside the realm of reason. *Is* there anything beyond the realm of human reason? Yes, I believe there is. Something.

In the meantime, here we all are together—I mean all of us people, not just alcoholics. We need each other.

New York, New York

CONVERSATION

I believe that the A.A. program is simply the will of God being put to practical, everyday use. And I think that the spiritual awakening is the realization that God will help the individual—if the individual is completely honest in his efforts.

If God were to enter my prison cell for a brief talk, our conversation might be as follows:

God: "I've had My eye on you for a long time, and I'm glad that you are finally trying to help yourself."

Myself: "I'm trying hard, but, truthfully, I am scared."

God: "You keep trying, and listen to the people that I have working for Me in A.A., and heed their advice. I have to leave now, for I have a busy itinerary. But if you need Me, I will always be near."

Waupun, Wisconsin

GOD IS GOOD

Before A.A., I could not, or would not, admit I was wrong. My pride would not let me. And yet I was ashamed of me. Caught in this conflict, I banished God from my life because I felt He asked me to adhere to a behavior pattern too high for a man of my human frailty. Somehow, I believed that there could be no forgiveness for *any* failure, that God required me to be *all* good. The moral of the story of the Prodigal Son eluded me.

Since I thought trying was not enough, I stopped trying. That made me feel guilty. For a while, alcohol blotted out the guilt. Then alcohol became the greatest cause of my guilt. I had to be beaten to a pulp physically, mentally, and emotionally, become bankrupt in all facets of my being, before I could give up my pride and admit defeat. Unfortunately, admitting was not sufficient. My situation got worse until I had to surrender completely. From the depths of my hell, I called out, "Oh God, help," and He led me to a place where I could find a way out of the maze and then sent me a group of people to lead the way.

I know that now. But at the time, I rejected God and claimed I did not believe in prayer. It took some time for my guides to get me to talk to God through prayer. Before then, I used the Fellowship of A.A. and the people in it as my higher power. They were real, compassionate, and understanding, and they made me feel welcome. But my distorted sense of justice told me there was no reason for God to forgive me, so I still felt ashamed and guilty when His name was mentioned.

When I gave up completely and accepted the nature of my disease, as well as the full meaning of the First Step, I had to have something bigger to tie to. The Fellowship as a higher power just was not enough. (I still use A.A. as a reminder that God exists, but I do not use it in place of God.) So, out of need, I came to believe.

To go along with this deep-seated belief in God, I have developed an enormous faith in God. He is good. My understanding is that *everything* He sends my way is for my benefit. But the growth of this understanding has taken time, as well as a relinquishing of my resistance to change. I needed the trials and tribulations I have had, so that I could surrender and give up self. Only in complete acceptance of the utter defeat of my pride and ego could I *begin* to win.

I am against goals which can be attained. People do not get married and live happily ever after. I could not dry out and live in Utopia. Each day, God gives us a new challenge. Sometimes, it is prosperity; sometimes, adversity. Prosperity can lead to complacency; adversity, to self-pity. Either one of these reactions is a luxury I cannot afford. I do not always fully accept my adversities as good while I am going through them, but the mere fact that I am now able to write these words proves the logic in my faith that God is good.

It is strictly my opinion, based on my experience, that one becomes richer in spirit as one grows in spirit. The more I accept God, the more He gives me. As I become more appreciative of the benefits received, I try harder to show my appreciation. My capacity to be content with life as it is has greatly increased. Therefore, as time goes on, I become more able to be at peace with my fellowman, with God, and within myself.

Deming, New Mexico

"THE WHOLE COMPANY OF . . ."

I was born an Anglican (Church of England), and the following crops up in one of our services (perhaps in the services of other denominations also): "Therefore with angels and archangels and the whole company of heaven, we laud and glorify Thy name." Since I have no knowledge of heaven or the company kept there, whenever I repeat this passage of praise, I substitute the words "and the whole company of Alcoholics Anonymous."

Being an A.A. Loner, I have felt very out of things and on my own. But I do believe in the power of collective thought, whether for good or evil. Thus, I believe that the collective thought of the body of Alcoholics Anonymous throughout the world must have some effect on alcoholics, whether they are aware of it or not.

Kenton-on-Sea, South Africa

GUIDING PRESENCE

In my early boyhood, reciting "Now I lay me down to sleep" and learning to sing "Jesus Loves Me" were part of my everyday life. Attending Sunday school and then church became an accepted one-day-a-week activity.

How much these things affected my life as a small boy, I really don't know, but at any time when I experienced fear or trouble, I always turned to a live adult for comfort and reassurance.

No doubt, some of these childhood teachings remained with me through the years, even after I came to depend on the bottle instead, for comfort in time of trouble and for an answer to my problems. But with increasing dependence on the bottle and the anguish, heartache, and loneliness that went with it, there seemed to be a sharp and total decline in all spiritual beliefs and feelings. I became a human paradox; in desperation, I would cry to God to help me out of this terrible mess; in the next breath, I would damn him for not helping me. On occasion, I would expound at great length to others that I was an atheist and did not believe there was a God—if there was, how could he let one of His own creations suffer so much and live in the hell that I was living in?

Each day became so painful that at last I turned, as a small, terrified child, to a living, sober, sane adult for comfort and help. He took me to a place where I had vowed I would never go, a meeting of Alcoholics Anonymous. When the meeting was opened with a moment of silence, I wondered why, but I was impressed. At the close of the meeting, I was shocked when they stood and began to repeat the Lord's Prayer. I tried to join them, though I had long ago forgotten the words. And again I was impressed. In spite of having been thoroughly inebriated a few hours earlier, I returned home feeling good. I seemed to understand that here at last was the hope and help I had been searching for. I fell into a deep, peaceful sleep that night while trying to recall the words of the Lord's Prayer.

That first day and for some weeks following, I had the comforting feeling of never being alone. During every minute of every day, this good, strong, guiding presence seemed to be always with me. I couldn't see it, yet it was there. Never once did I tell anyone of this experience I was having, for I was convinced they would say that it was but a figment of my imagination and that, if I would just bear with it, my sanity would return in time. I wasn't so sure myself that there might not be something wrong with my mind. Even so, I was delighted with what was happening to me, and I wanted it to continue. If this was a sign of insanity, I thought, let me remain forever in its grasp.

One day, I suddenly realized that this great invisible Something or Someone was no longer by my side. I felt momentarily lonely—until I reasoned that this Someone greater than myself had decided it was now time for me to face the new realities of a new life. But should I need some help along the way, I felt that He would always be close by, as the small child who crosses the street alone for the first time knows that his mother is watching from the window. When, through these personal experiences, I came to believe that the divine Architect had laid out a master plan that included me, in my own small way, I found that I had a certain degree of sustaining faith to cope with everyday living in a sane and confident manner.

Grand Island, Nebraska

A LIVING PART OF A.A.

God is a living part of A.A. I feel His presence each time I look into the concerned eyes around me. His greatest commandment is "Love thy neighbor as thyself." This seems to me to be the entire purpose of A.A.

Marysville, Ohio

SPIRITUAL
PROGRESS

9

We are not saints.
The point is that we are
willing to grow along spiritual
lines. The principles we have set down
are guides to progress. We claim
spiritual progress rather than
spiritual perfection.

Bill W.

"Alcoholics Anonymous," page 60

DESTINATIONS

Only Twelve Steps. In a day when we are exposed to fantastic statistics, a mere dozen doesn't seem to rate much. But what is involved in the Twelve Steps makes a great difference.

I can remember how thrilled my wife and I were when we saw each of our twins take the first step at eleven months. Soon, it was two steps, then three, then four, and in no time at all there was no way of counting the steps they had taken. They were free—free to go on and on.

That first step is very important, whether it is the first step of a beloved child learning to walk—or the First Step, taken by a man on his way to a new life. Looking into my little ones' faces, I can see the same qualities that we need for the Twelve Steps of A.A.: daring, to stake everything on the attempt; a sense of direction, to be followed with no swerving, no detour; decision, to move forward without hesitation or reservation; determination, to make it all the way. Destination: a full life, a free life, a serene life.

Albany, Australia

TOTALLY FREE

After eleven years' sobriety, one day at a time, I have growing awareness of how incredibly blessed I am. At first, it was all I could manage to stay sober that one day. I never allowed myself an excuse to miss an A.A. meeting, and I read all the A.A. Conference-approved literature I could buy or borrow. I also read other publications, such as William James's "The Varieties of Religious Experience" (because Bill W. did). I read several daily devotionals (and still do, including my precious "24 Hours a Day"). I attended confirmation classes in my church to review the Christian teaching of my youth, from which I had become so far removed

Growth and understanding came slowly, but they came steadily. And finally, I could feel gratitude for my sobriety—for the saving grace of God. Now I feel totally free, because I know the truth about myself. I learned about *people* in A.A., and this brought me to an understanding of myself. I know that spiritual growth is a great, wide, beautiful thing and that I have only stepped up to the open door.

By going to meetings and rubbing elbows with the new people in A.A., I find they have much to teach me. Their problems are a little different, and they haven't experienced the awful isolation that many of us older folks did. But they are better informed; they are more knowledgeable; and I suspect they are smarter, because they learn faster. Perhaps they don't have as far to go to get well as we did, but their path is more cluttered, and the way isn't as clear. So it is still the same struggle for all of us, and we need each other. We need each other's experience, strength, and hope, regardless of age or length of sobriety.

The saving grace of God doesn't come like a bolt out of the blue. It comes through, in, and from other suffering, as well as rescued, souls like you and me.

I am happy to be part of a living and growing fellowship with an infallible heartbeat. Divine power is the pulse of A.A., and it doesn't change, no matter how errant and foolish we mortals be.

Bismarck, North Dakota

THE WONDER OF DISCOVERIES

I wanted to be the most "successful" member of my A.A. group. But it was a long time before I could think clearly. I stayed sober largely through fear and the thrill of trying to carry the message. I would talk frequently and at length on the value of "working the Steps" and "living this new way of Life." Unfortunately, that's all I did about it—just talk. I did not really attempt to take the Steps.

Instead, I tried to find spiritual help and peace of mind through my church. For this activity, I felt certain that I would be rewarded with good health and happiness. It didn't work.

Although I never took another drink, my general health declined. I became highly nervous and tense. As a result, an ulcer, high blood pressure, and acute neuritis finally took me to the hospital, where I lay almost blind, crippled, and near death.

After my doctors had determined the chief medical cause for my illness, they predicted that I would live after all. Then I had much time to think and to meditate. I reviewed my entire life—the years before

A.A. and the twelve years in A.A. Somehow, I felt free to look objectively at what I had been and what I had become. For the first time in my life, it grew quite clear to me that I was an utter, complete, 100-percent, dyed-in-the-wool louse. I was so self-centered, so full of ego, that I had all but destroyed myself. During the years in A.A., I had learned little more than to "keep the plug in the jug." I had neglected to try to work *all* the Twelve Steps of the program.

But it occurred to me that now God had twice saved me from self-destruction. I began to feel a sense of real gratitude, and I tried to thank Him. I had a strong feeling that God had spared me for a purpose. To express my gratitude, I wanted to spend the rest of my life trying to help someone else, and I knew that one of the best places to work was in the Fellowship of Alcoholics Anonymous, without my old, shallow ideas of "success."

I discovered the satisfaction of helping to arrange the chairs for a meeting or of cleaning the ashtrays. Soon, I discovered that A.A. service work can be most rewarding, and I loved doing it. Yes, I did go back and start all over on the Twelve Steps, and I felt the wonder of other discoveries—about myself and my Higher Power. I would have felt this years ago had I but followed the program and had I been, as the Big Book states, "willing to go to any length to get it."

A.A. today affords me the privilege of being at ease in a world of "normal" people. It gives me the opportunity to try to live and work in my church and community, and perhaps in these areas, too, offer a small contribution toward making things just a little bit better for those yet to come.

Cordell, Oklahoma

EVIDENCE OF A MIRACLE

My alcoholism was not far advanced when I first sought the help of A.A., but the effects of thirty years of drinking were there, and my spiritual life was at a low ebb. All desire to drink left me at my first meeting, and, believing, I took to the program with enthusiasm, minded the slogans, went to meetings, made friends, and carried the message as I understood it then.

Shortly after joining A.A., I underwent a religious conversion. I had been a Christian just nominally—about as ill-informed on spiritual matters in general as one can imagine. Upon truly discovering Christianity, I studied theology in its many branches, became a lay member of a religious order, and was a daily communicant. I felt secure. so I drifted away from the Fellowship, no longer participated in meetings, lost track of my A.A. friends, and became extremely "busy."

When I took a drink, after thirteen years of sobriety, I am sure I had in mind that A.A. would still be there if the result proved dire. Surprisingly, the whiskey had no apparent effect. For a couple of years after that, I would have an occasional drink. My life situation was entirely different from what it had been fifteen years before; gradually, deceiving myself skillfully, I became convinced that I had been mistaken about my alcoholism. For a few years, I managed to appear to be a social drinker. There were portents to the contrary, but I ignored them. I cherished my illusion of control.

The deterioration of my spiritual life was slow; the physical and mental effects were not especially noticeable for quite a while. Inevitably, the time came when I faced the fact that I could neither cut down on the considerable amount I was drinking, nor could I stop. In desperation, I had myself hospitalized. My chart read "acute alcoholism," and I suffered all the symptoms, including hallucinations. Yet after release I continued to drink, completely obsessed.

One day, my doctor suggested that I go into the hospital again. I said I would think about it. A friend came for tea that day (my tea was more than half vodka) and said, just in passing, "You know, dear, it isn't worth it." Just that.

After she left, the words "It isn't worth it" kept running through my mind. The next morning, I phoned the local A.A. intergroup office and asked for a meeting list. I have not had a drink since that day.

Now I see how monumental my self-deception was. During that first thirteen years, my sobriety was not of the high quality it seemed to be. During the two years that followed, I actually convinced myself that it was a privilege to be able to drink. When I returned to A.A., its precepts seemed entirely new to me, particularly the full meaning of the First Step, the "atom bomb of the program." Instead of taking the Steps and forgetting them, this time I began living them daily, finding new meaning in each one.

What I have come to believe is profound, and my concept and understanding of the program are quite different from what they were before. My A.A. way of life now demands constant action—an active self-honesty and recognition of the necessity for living in day-tight compartments. Patience must be practiced. In gratitude, I must humbly come to believe every moment of every day. Each day, I must surrender and rededicate my life, or I shall lose all that I have gained ⸀ nave always believed in God, but I must never again forget how easy it is to lose contact and to become again "unsane."

"I sought my soul, but my soul I could not see. I sought my God, but my God eluded me. I sought my brother, and I found all three." We find our brothers in the Fellowship, and therein lies spiritual strength. Your understanding of God may be quite different from mine, but we may agree, I think, that there is a Holy Spirit pervading A.A. meetings and that the sobriety of each and every one of us is evidence of a miracle.

A miracle is defined as an event that appears unexplainable and so is held to be supernatural in origin—an act of God. This I accept. David Stewart has written: "A miracle is an astonishing action, emerging from the concerted effort of God and a person." I agree—and in A.A. "a person" becomes many people. A.A. succeeds because, one and all, we have a common goal toward which we are working: mental, emotional, and spiritual growth, through love and service. Once we come to believe, we are given the opportunity to work toward this goal.

For me, coming to believe is not a one-time experience. It is an action to be performed daily as long as I live and grow.

New York, New York

ONLY ONE REASON

I believe we are all sober and alive for only one reason: God has a job for us to do. I have also come to believe that I must please God first, myself second, and everybody else third. When I can live and feel that way—and it isn't all day every day—things seem to work out. When *I* try to run the show, everything goes to hell.

Akron, Ohio

THE CENTRAL EXPERIENCE

I make no claim that I know God in all His fullness. And I certainly don't feel that I understand God to any extent. But that there is a power beyond my personal will which can do wonderful, friendly things for me that I can't do for myself—this I know beyond all question. I have felt this marvelous healing power at work in my own being, and I have seen the miraculous effects of this mysterious, indefinable power in the lives of thousands of recovering addicts who are my friends in Alcoholics Anonymous.

For over twenty years, I was an atheist or an agnostic. During that time, I became a helpless alcoholic and an amphetamine addict and a complete failure in all areas of my life. All of my horrible suffering was self-induced. And during those proud years, I often said, "If God exists, let Him give me a sign." I had quite forgotten that I was the one who had broken off communication, when I became very clever during my seventeenth year. At that time, I set out to prove that there was no God, and for over twenty years, the confirmations of my opinion kept pouring in. So the first thing that I came to understand about God is that *He is very cooperative.* It took me twenty years of suffering to learn this!

The second thing I learned is that *God is love.* One of the saints says, "Every man that loveth is born of God." It was my good fortune to spend my first day in A.A. with such a man. He attended three meetings with me that day, and took me to his home for both lunch and dinner. I was bewildered and confused; I felt that if he had really known me, he would not have had me in his home. His love and acceptance alone did not bring me into the program. I had been offered love and encouragement and advice and understanding many times before. But this time I responded! We are not healed by love alone, but by our response to love. *Our understanding of God grows through our willing response to Him.*

My sponsor said, "Pray if you can." Having no faith whatever, thinking that prayer must be a kind of autohypnotic play-acting, alone in my apartment I got down on my knees like a little child and prayed to the unknown God. I said, "God, take away my compulsion to drink." And my compulsion to drink was removed, and it has not returned from that day to this. Without knowing how I had done it, I had surrendered to the Power, and the Power did for me what I could not do of my own will.

I went to an A.A. meeting every night, and every night I prayed, and every night I had long, wonderful dream conversations with God. "The central experience," as I now often call it, was enfolding me and drawing me in as perfectly as my disordered mind would permit. I had been given great gifts—the gift of faith and the confirmation of faith—and I became so excited that I couldn't make up my mind whether to found a new religion or run for pope.

For about three months, I went to meetings and prayed and dreamed and procrastinated. The pink cloud faded, and I began to feel very uncomfortable at times, and I was told that I was ready to do something about tidying up the refuse from the past. The next thing I learned about God is that *"Faith without works is dead."*

Gradually, I began applying myself to Steps Four through Nine, and after about four years, the power of the past to hurt me was largely removed. *I came to believe in a God who was merciful and forgiving, but not forgetful.* And *I* have no desire to forget the past. My memories no longer fill me with shame and remorse. On the contrary, they fill me with gratitude and joy. My whole story is a sort of divine mystery to me. I don't know how an intelligent human being ever could have got into such a mess, and the more firmly established in sanity I become, the more amazed I am that I ever got out of the mess.

Very early in my A.A. life, I realized that the experience of God and the concept of God had not been invented by A.A.'s. For me, it was not enough merely to rely upon my own experiences and continue to repeat the words "God as I understand Him" at meetings. I rediscovered the God of the Bible largely through the practice of techniques described by Norman Vincent Peale in his "The Power of Positive Thinking." I became confirmed in the church of my choice and made my peace with the God of my childhood. I learned that the fearful God I had imagined as a child was really a God of love.

But the record of religious institutions generally began to appear to me more and more like my own: very high in promise and very low in performance. So I became interested in Christian mysticism, which led me into the study of techniques of deep meditation and of comparative religions. I began to realize that the so-called mystics of whatever tradition—Christian, Jewish, Buddhist, Hindu, Taoist, or Muhammadan —all ultimately talked the same language. In one way or another, they all described the same blissful One behind the Many, who could be directly known in deep prayer and meditation.

I began to meditate morning and evening, and the results were so startling that I felt the need for personal guidance. Vivid waking dreams and strange inner experiences made me a bit anxious about proceeding alone. I investigated the organizations in Toronto which taught meditation techniques, and I chose the society which appealed to me most.

What opinions I may hold, what techniques I may use one year or five years from now, I have no way of knowing. But I have noticed, during the past seven years, that I have always been happiest when my commitment to A.A. and its Twelve Steps has been greater than my involvement in any other activity or group.

In my present life from day to day, I attempt to improve my understanding of God by responding to Him in three basic ways: by moving outwards into positive action, by exercising my ability to choose positive thoughts, and by allowing myself to be drawn inwards to positive being.

For me, positive action means consciously trying to act towards other people in accordance with the scriptural teachings in which I believe, whether I feel like acting that way or not. I have found that it is much easier to act my way toward belief than it is to believe my way toward action. One of my daily action paths toward God is the path of fellowship in A.A. The great tragedy of the addict is that, of all the personality types, his is probably most in need of love, but gradually, through his addiction, he becomes totally unlovable. The loving fellowship of A.A. began my recovery, and I maintain daily contact with those who love me and understand me, for I need it almost as much now as when I attended my first meeting.

Another sort of path toward God which I try to follow every day is the process of positive thinking. A.A. taught me that it is actually possible—though not always easy—to stop a negative or despairing train of thought and, by the use of a repeated slogan, recover a sense of gratitude, which permits me to begin a positive train of thought. The ultimate positive thought, of course, is "God," the word which affirms our faith that the universe is friendly to our being.

Through prayer, I take the path of faith toward God. Every morning, I turn my will and my life over to the care of my God as I understand Him. His integrating power within me has gradually led me into a state of serenity and happiness which I had always considered impossible.

Through deep meditation, I take the effortless path toward God. I meditate for half an hour every morning and evening. The purpose of transcendental deep meditation is to allow the attention to be led deep within the mind to the source of thought, which is experienced as blissful being, and to bring the blissful nature of that state out into normal waking consciousness for enjoyment throughout the day.

I have become more and more aware of the infinite expansion of happiness which is accessible within. The Upanishad, part of the Hindu scriptures, concludes: "From Joy all things are born; by Joy all things are sustained; to Joy all things return." The more thoroughly I can surrender to this proposition, the more thoroughly I enjoy my life. Ultimately, my God as I understand Him is joy and the expansion of joy.

Toronto, Ontario

ANOTHER HELMSMAN

For years, my favorite literature was Homer: "The Odyssey" because all life is a journey; "The Iliad" because all life is a battle. Now I ask myself: But need life be as Homer seems to have seen it? Why should I be constantly journeying, running away from myself? Constantly battling myself and resisting or resenting this life that God has granted me? Why not relax and let Someone who is far more capable than I do the steering and planning?

Seattle, Washington

I MUST LEARN

Many in our Fellowship express our three stages of learning and growth this way: "I came. I came to. I came to believe."

In my case, it was about three years before the third stage began. Over the years since, I believe I have experienced a gradual strengthening and growth of frequency in my communication with God as I understand Him.

"Man is ready to die for an idea, provided that idea is not quite clear to him," Paul Eldridge wrote. That is the way the spiritual side of the A.A. program appears to me. I'm in trouble if I attempt to parse it; I don't attempt to understand it. These random notes represent the best I can do to put it into words:

Cardinal Newman said, "It is thy very energy of thought which keeps thee from thy God." So it was with me, I think. The saying "Let go and let God" must have been written just for me. . . .

For me, God is that still, quiet voice I hear so many times each day, saying, "Roy, that wasn't good enough!" . . .

I live alone. And once I was lonely. But now I can enjoy the rewards that come only in moments of solitude. . . .

I often protest against things that I look on as limitations and obstructions. But these could be the very things I need most. For what I call hindrances, obstacles, or discouragements are probably God's opportunities. . . .

As I try to grow in this A.A. program, I must occasionally "remember when"—but not in order to brood about the past. A.A. taught me how to deal with it, how to put it in its proper place and perspective. I believe that I must learn, that I must let God teach me, that the only way to get rid of my past is to get a future out of it. God will waste nothing. . . .

Now that I am sober and have tried to turn my will and life over to the care of God, I believe that the greatest gift I can bestow—upon the world or upon any one group of persons or upon any person in the world—is my own self. I think God gave each of us a unique personality, so that we in turn might give it to others. Now I *can* give it, with joy in life, warm, friendly, happy, sober! . . .

I believe that God made us all different for another reason: I am convinced that there is some one thing that I can do better than anyone else in this world. God thinks so. And he wants me to do it! Through the Twelve Steps, a good many A.A. members have found out what *their* assigned chores on earth are. And they are doing them.

Thus, the Twelve Steps must continue to be more compelling to me and more binding on me than anything else that I encounter in life. For only through working on these Steps can I get closer and closer to finding out God's intent for me.

Perhaps God thinks that a very modest task in my community is all that I am capable of. But it is there. It is real. And so, with the help of my friends in A.A., I must search out what that task is. Then, with their help, I must *do* it!

Toronto, Ontario

SOURCE OF STRENGTH

A few years before coming to A.A., I knew I was going crazy. I do remember crying out to God to help me. Somehow, I got the strength to leave my husband. (I was afraid that, on one of my violent drunks, I would kill him or be killed by him.) It was a long road from that moment to the time that I was able to get help and to know that God was in my life.

I had the first glimmer of hope at my first A.A. meeting. My fear was that I might not have the disease of alcoholism; if I didn't, I knew I would never make it. Life had ceased to function for me in any normal way; my depressions were paralyzing.

A.A. seemed to present to me the direction and structure I had longed for. I began to have just the slightest motivation and just the slightest will to live. Through months of painful withdrawnness and hostility, I slowly began to find a voice within me that had to be heard. I forced myself to speak up at a meeting, so I could prove to myself that I existed. Then I began to get some freedom, but I was not really connecting. I had found friends in A.A., and it became a family for me, but after a while this wasn't enough. In facing life for the first time, I was full of fear. I could discuss problems with these friends and with doctors, but there was an ingredient missing in my life.

Always before, I had put myself in the hands of a man and made him the sole reason for my existence and my will to live. I knew that if I did this again, my disillusionment would be hard to bear. I had to have my *own* will to live. And this perhaps is when I began to rely on God—Someone to protect me, Someone who wouldn't possess me, Someone I could silently talk to and pray to. Perhaps I became willing to believe.

I would tell a friend of mine, who was having the same problems, that I prayed to God not to take a drink today and not to get married today. It was a sort of pact. I was very serious about this. I couldn't seem to handle romance and God too well at the same time. And God did start to give me the strength that I had always thought would come from the man in my life.

I need power each day, because I get weary. But with A.A. as my structure and God as my source of strength, I can face life without taking a drink. I don't have to stare out my window in total despair any more. The ocean and the sun and the trees and all the fantastic beauty that God has created have finally become very real to me. I crave and need the presence of nature. But I must also bear in mind that it is the spirit within me, which comes from God, that is going to be the healing force. I can turn to it wherever I am.

I want very much to share myself with another human being now. I am afraid of taking that step. But, then, I have been afraid of everything else, too, and now I know that it is possible to overcome fear.

New York, New York

CHANGING BELIEFS

When I arrived, trembling and terrified, at my first meeting, I thought I no longer believed in anything. What a miracle that, after one talk with my sponsor and one meeting, I could have hope in A.A.! This hope kept me coming to meetings and gradually grew into a true belief that A.A. had all the answers for me, that, if I would be willing and try, I could stay sober—one day at a time. However, I found that this involved the effort to practice the program.

Once my belief in A.A. had been established, it became apparent that all Twelve Steps were important to my continuing sobriety. But I was stymied on the Third Step, with its reference to "the care of God." So I went around it, knowing I must return to it, and tackled the Fourth Step. Slowly and painfully, I became aware of myself. I began to see it wasn't true that I didn't believe in anything. Rather, I had believed in the wrong things:

I had believed I needed a drink for confidence.
I had believed I was unattractive.
I had believed I was unworthy.
I had believed no one loved me.
I had believed I never had a break.

Someone said at a closed meeting, "There is good in all of us. Seek it out, nurture it, tend it, and it will flourish." So I began searching for the positives within me. I realized that my feeling of inferiority was just one aspect of ego, and the arrogance I projected was the other. I must find the center median. So I tried to *act as if*:

A.A. was giving me confidence.

I had an attractive personality, even though I was not beautiful.

I was worthy, like all others.

I loved myself and could therefore love others.

Faith was freeing me from the fear that had always gripped me.

Now I believed, at least, that I *could* become whole with the tools of the A.A. program: pursuing the Steps, reading A.A. literature, asking questions at closed meetings, latching on to older A.A.'s who had that mysterious quality of serenity. I discovered that all those whom I emulated and admired had put the Third Step into their lives. I knew I wanted to do likewise.

This necessitated my finding a God of my understanding, plus a willingness to let go. I realized that I must say, "Thy will be done." But who or what was this "Thy" to me? I began to go back, to review. What *had* I come to believe?

I had come to believe in the A.A. program.

I had come to believe that a power (A.A.) greater than myself could restore me to sanity.

I had come to believe that I no longer needed a drink.

I had come to believe that I could grow to be a whole person.

I had come to believe that faith could eliminate fear.

I had come to believe that I could love myself and so love others.

I had come to believe that love was the key.

With an open heart, I returned to the Third Step and turned my will and my life over to the care of the God of my understanding.

Fort Lauderdale, Florida

"IN ALL OUR AFFAIRS"

10

*Service gladly rendered, obligations
squarely met, troubles well accepted or
solved with God's help, the
knowledge that at home or in the world
outside we are partners in a common
effort, the fact that in God's sight all
human beings are important, the proof
that love freely given brings a full
return, the certainty that we are no longer
isolated and alone in self-constructed
prisons, the surety that we can fit and
belong in God's scheme of things—these
are the satisfactions of right living
for which no pomp and circumstance, no
heap of material possessions, could
possibly be substitutes.*

Bill W.

"Twelve Steps and Twelve Traditions," page 124

WE WALK THIS WAY

After nearly ten years of sitting on bar stools, backing away from jobs, and running from people, I brought me and my drinking problem to Alcoholics Anonymous. It was not the most thrilling end that I could think of for a newly married young woman, but I had to admit that an unmanageable life would not be helpful to the baby I was expecting.

Still, since my husband had joined A.A. before we met, life seemed to be really complete once I became part of the Fellowship, too. I had been sober three months when our first child was born. One year and one month later, the second child arrived. Our third "A.A. baby" was born one year and four months after the second. So my progress in A.A. was marked by three little girls. I couldn't imagine anyone feeling more fulfilled than I did on the third anniversary of my sobriety.

Then came a turning point. All of a sudden, I felt completely at odds with the A.A. way of life. A doctor confirmed our worst fears when he announced that something was seriously wrong with our youngest child. Muscular dystrophy was suspected, but hospital studies disproved that diagnosis. We were left with a vague definition of our little girl's problem; the doctors who had been called for consultation categorized her disability under the heading of cerebral palsy. None offered hope for her recovery, and an orthopedic specialist told us flatly that our daughter would never walk.

In the face of one pessimistic prediction after another, I wilted. Certainly, I knew that this was a time when my daughter needed whatever strength her mother could muster. I seemed to have none. My husband retained his faith; he had a positive belief that the doctors would prove to be mistaken. He never doubted that our daughter would walk.

Our A.A. friends also had this positive belief in the child's recovery. They did their best to revive my fast-dying energies, and these positive forces of loving faith caused me to reassess my progress in the A.A. program. I was sober, but had I turned my will over to the care of

God as I understood Him? What was I doing about "conscious contact" with my Higher Power? Was the Tenth Step part of my daily life or only a once-tried effort?

Most of the answers were negative. This meant that, while my daughter might be in a hopeless situation physically, I was functioning in a way destined to retard any progress she might make spiritually and mentally. There was no other solution than to get out of the child's way and work on myself.

In the years that followed, my A.A. activity was increased. I reached out for my Higher Power—God—as I had never reached before. Then, one day, our daughter walked! I had accidentally let go of her hand. Our reaction to this was the same as the reaction of the people in the Scripture to the lame man's walking—"wonder and amazement."

At this point, she is twelve years old, and medical authorities have called her progress "unprecedented." I am still haunted by a neurologist's statement that her coordination is controlled by her mental processes. So long as her spirit remains free and alert, her physical activity is enthusiastic and unhampered. When her spirit is dampened, activity falters. What better lesson could I need?

This child is my textbook on "How It Works." From the day that I let go mentally to the day that I let go physically, she progressed beyond anyone's fondest dreams and hopes. I now try to follow her lead in working my A.A. program. As a profound thinker once said, "Self-reliance is ultimately reliance on God." How can this truth be denied when personal experience shows it to be so?

Philadelphia, Pennsylvania

FROM LONELINESS TO SOLITUDE

"I'm lonely—I'm lonely!" is the cry of drinking alcoholics all over the face of the earth—in a lonely room, in a crowded bar, in the heart of a family gathering, on a street in the midst of hundreds of people. Then, in contradiction, people would get on our nerves and we would go off by ourselves to "get away from it all." But this didn't work, either; we could not endure for long the burden of our dark thoughts.

We tried hard to remove our aloneness with the bottle, and for a little while we could, but not for long. When we hit bottom and realized we could not go on as we were, by the grace of God we found ourselves thrust into an unbearable aloneness, separated from everything and everybody. Thus separated, we were able to look at our lives, our problem, the hopelessness of our situation. Only now could we ask questions and give answers and make decisions. Now we could make a decision to do something about our drinking *and living* problems.

There are two sides of man's being alone. In our language, "loneliness" expresses the pain of being alone. "Solitude" expresses the glory of being alone.

What happens to us in A.A. that makes it possible for us, not only to endure, but to enjoy moments of solitude? What changes our loneliness to solitude?

The love and understanding we find in A.A. are a protective curtain between ourselves and the aching aloneness of our drinking days. The first few weeks, some of us spend most of our time in an A.A. club talking with others. Then it becomes evident that we must go to work and somehow meet the demands and responsibilities of our daily lives. We are afraid. Will the old loneliness hit us again when we are out of the actual presence of other A.A. members?

Sooner or later, by practicing the principles of the Twelve Steps, we find in ourselves a very precious thing, something inside that we can be comfortable with regardless of whether we are at home by ourselves or anywhere else that life takes us.

A.A. members are not emotional cripples who need someone to hold their hands every moment of the day and night to prevent their falling. We grow up with the help of God, as we understand Him, and the fellowship of the group, and by applying the Twelve Steps to our lives.

As the sober weeks go by, we can enjoy and treasure the few moments of solitude we are able to find in the rush and hurry of life today. When we cease to fear loneliness and begin to cherish and use our solitude to advantage, we have come a long way. We realize a little solitude is necessary to think and to try to work some of the Steps. In solitude, we take our inventories. In solitude, we admit to ourselves the exact nature of our wrongs. In solitude, our spirits seek that Power greater than we are; in solitude, we seek through prayer and meditation to be aware of God's will for us.

Solitude can be sought and experienced in many ways—in the silence of nature, in reading poetry, in listening to music, in looking at pictures, and in sincere thoughtfulness. We are alone, but not lonely. Yet these experiences cannot answer all the questions in our minds. So we return to the world of man.

Some of us long to become creative in some realm of life. But we cannot become or remain creative without solitude. One hour of *conscious* solitude will enrich our creativity far more than hours of trying to learn the creative process.

Solitude is not easy; sometimes, we can find it only by remaining silent and allowing our souls to sigh without words to God. This we can do even in a crowded day and a crowded room, even under the most difficult external conditions. No one can take these moments from us. The center of our being, the innermost self that is the ground of our aloneness, is elevated to the divine center and taken into it. Only in a movement that rises first to God and then returns from Him to the other person can we find communion with others.

Even love is reborn in solitude, for only in solitude can those who are alone reach those from whom they are separated. One hour of solitude may bring us closer to those we love than many hours of communication. We can take them with us to the "hills of eternity."

Houston, Texas

HAPPINESS

To arrive at a working definition of happiness in my attempts to apply the blueprint of A.A. to rebuilding a shattered life, I tried first to recall the happiness we chased in the old days. I suspect that for most of us happiness was equated with bliss.

In booze we reached for euphoria, release from even the faintest threat of responsibility. We wanted insulation against the urgent clanging of the world around us, a soft berth on a languid cloud. And for fleeting moments, just before the curtain of oblivion cranked down, we did drift into that never-never state.

Then they said, "Come into A.A. We'll help you maintain sobriety, and you'll know *real* happiness."

The sobriety was real, but suddenly so was the world—a harsh and pitiless place we had never fully faced before. Where was this highly touted stuff called happiness?

A latter-day philosopher has said that happiness is not something we experience; it is something we remember. Still, at the risk of sounding unfashionable, I'll say, "I *am* very happy." Let me hasten to add that none of what I now possess came easy. For me, it has been and is a tough grind. Relinquishing the prerogatives of chronic brattery never comes easy. But early in the game I needed definitions.

"Serenity," a word we've used from the moment we struggled into our first A.A. meeting, was from the start a tricky one. It seems to mean anything from Sanforized, snag-proof, fully guaranteed bliss to the ability to maintain a stiff upper lip when things don't go our way. I have heard the Serenity Prayer chanted as an incantation to wield a spell against temptation, a wand to wave away all unpleasantness. For what it's worth, my own definition of serenity evolved somewhat like this:

It appears to me that most of the wrenching turmoil in people's lives—whether or not they are alcoholic—derives from too stubborn persistence in trying to resolve *insoluble* problems. That is why the philosophy contained in the Serenity Prayer is one of the most important guidelines I've found in A.A.

Accept the things you cannot change. So simple. If the problem cannot be solved—*today*—why, simply drop it. I grant that this is not always easy; it takes self-discipline, a faculty infrequently found in newly sober alcoholics.

On the other hand, problems which *can* be solved provide the real excitement in life. The daily challenge to grapple with and master the conflicts encountered from dawn to dark is stimulating.

But the last line of the Serenity Prayer contains the clinker—the *wisdom* to know the difference between soluble and insoluble situations. As one who is most suspicious of his wisdom (since sobering up, anyway), I find that substituting the word "honesty" for "wisdom" often furnishes the clue to the answer I'm seeking.

The second tenet of the Serenity Prayer is too frequently slurred over. I am constantly amazed at the number of so-called obstacles I have overcome after giving them a *second* look, mustering what meager resources I have, then taking the hoe in hand.

Serenity to me, therefore, is *the absence of insoluble conflict.* And it is up to me first to determine whether, after an honest look at myself, I can cope with the problem, then to decide whether it is to be tackled, passed over to another day, or dismissed forever.

We can establish goals with realistic horizons—if we maintain rigorously honest recognition of our limitations. Winning the daily skirmishes involved in achieving these goals is exciting. These are the real kicks.

The Charles Addams house I am attempting to rebuild will never be the Taj Mahal, but it will be my own handiwork, with all its quirks of do-it-yourself and built-in bloodstains and bloopers of enthusiasm unrelieved by any real talent in this department.

I will never grow tomatoes the size of my neighbor's, but my puny little produce tastes better on my table than his beauties would.

For the first time, I am giving an employer a fair shake, and I know the warmth and satisfaction of working on a team, of contributing my tiny share to a successful whole.

The only gallery my paintings will ever adorn runs between our living room and the front hall, but dabbling in a new field is fun and the things are improving, even if I'm the only one who can see the change.

Our school budget was defeated, but at least I had the satisfaction of knowing we put up a good fight. (Imagine even being interested in such a thing in the old days!) Wait until next year.

I barely knew the family I lost to booze. My present wife and children, direct dividends of sobriety, give me the greatest joy. Never in my life, before A.A., had I really done anything *for* anyone. Yet even today I can't quite catch up, for I still receive more than I can ever give.

There is only one thing as beautiful as the face of a four-year-old boy at story-telling time, and that is the face of his little sister.

So happiness to me is fulfillment, the satisfaction gained from knowing that you did the best your honestly evaluated limitations would permit—in all phases of living.

Happiness is gratitude for the miracle which granted another go-around at a life once abandoned.

Happiness is growing up. It is learning to recognize all the things you really have. Happiness is for experiencing, as well as remembering.

New Hartford, New York

A LESSON IN HUMILITY

God, as I understand Him, has a sense of humor. One of the incidents that proved this to me happened in May, when I was asked to say a few words at our church service on Mother's Day.

As soon as I began thinking about it, "a few words" became a sermon. After a few short hours, the sermon (which still had to be written) became one of the best sermons ever heard in our church. In a few days, as I started working on the sermon, it became probably the best sermon ever heard in North Bay. And as the week passed, it was quite possible that I would be asked to give several other sermons in our church. As a result, of course, people from other churches would come to hear me. I thought it quite likely that later on people from other places—even as far away as Sault Ste. Marie—would be flocking to hear me!

Less than five years earlier, one of my major fears had been that I would die and not one soul would attend my funeral.

When the moment for my "sermon" actually arrived, God in His mercy and wisdom stepped in. I developed the most awful thirst, beyond anything I'd ever suffered when I was drinking. I started my talk, but had to keep interrupting it every second sentence or so to take a drink. The water didn't quench that thirst. And soon, as the thirst deepened, I was drinking more than I was talking. I felt an almost overwhelming temptation to toast the congregation with a "Here's mud in your eye" toss of the glass.

And then the light came on. Then the message came through. God was telling me, "You are an alcoholic. That is all you are. Not a preacher, not a teacher, not a speaker. Just an alcoholic, recovering by My grace."

And that was that. A lesson taught with humor. A lesson I must never forget: The important thing is not what I do or where I live or what my name is; the important thing is that I am a recovering alcoholic, by the grace of God, through membership in A.A.

North Bay, Ontario

GETTING AHEAD

Most alcoholics I have known, including myself, wanted to get ahead. If we didn't, well, there was nothing so rosy as the dreams of success and glory which subsequently came out of the bottle; such fantasies are the warp and woof of the active alcoholic's life.

I think that one of the main differences between an active alcoholic and a recovering alcoholic can be expressed as a matter of tense. The active alcoholic tends to live in the future or in the past. The sober alcoholic, using part of the philosophy he learns in his A.A. experience, lives or strives to live in the present.

The nondrinking alcoholic discovers in A.A. that you cannot Get Ahead until you learn to be Here. We discover from our Serenity Prayer that one of the things we cannot change is time. The Here-and-Now is the only reality, whereas in the unreal world of the drinking alcoholic there was only yesterday-and-tomorrow.

The grace of sobriety lies in accepting the fact that the past is nonexistent and the future exists only in the present.

I think of a certain morning on which I woke up and said to myself I would not take a drink that day. I had done this many times before, and each time I had failed. But on this morning, for some unaccountable reason, another voice told me I was a liar; that I couldn't *not* take a drink that day. Immediately, the stage was set for what was, to put it mildly, the most unusual day of my life: the day on which my compulsion for alcohol was taken from me.

The explanation is simple. When I said to myself, "You are a liar," I was thinking in the present. I didn't say, "If you go through the morning and take a drink in the afternoon, you *will* be a liar." Right then, I was empowered to do something about my predicament, because I recognized it as a present predicament and not a future one. So I sought A.A. and found the help I needed. In the very moment of acknowledging myself to be a liar, I turned out not to be one (in that instance, anyhow).

Ever since I became extricated from the turmoil of alcoholic living, it has interested me to muse over this business of Getting Ahead. In the excesses of my alcohol-inspired ambition, I used to imagine that to Get Ahead I would need to be like some preternatural bulldozer, plowing its way upward and onward, plunging inexorably over the embankments of life, grinding, heaving, snorting, reckless of obstacles, impelled by the virtues of ambition and the seductions of success—the kind of success that comes effortlessly to us from a barroom bottle.

I did not know then that if you want to Get Ahead with any degree of peace, you must first learn to Stay Here. It takes guts to Stay Here; it takes self-discipline and resolution. Anyone with sufficient energy and a one-track mind can Get Ahead; witness the robber barons, the dictators, the demagogues. But to Stay Here, you must know where you are before you can know where you are going. You must seek before you can find, and you must ask before you really learn to seek. It takes humility to ask, patience to wait for the answer, and faith that the answer will come. These, it strikes me, are hardly bulldozer "virtues."

I like to think that Staying Here provides a clue to the practice of the Eleventh Step. We don't improve our conscious contact with God, as we understand Him, by projecting into the future. After all, even the Hereafter begins with Here.

Manchester, Massachusetts

A PRACTICAL PHILOSOPHY

By being in the environment of A.A., I've been sober for over eight years. And I've received help from a lot of practical philosophy—a way of thinking that produces real results.

"Made a decision to turn our will and our lives over to the care of God *as we understood Him.*" The Third Step can be a tough order, particularly if one is not very religious or if one has some problems in the "God" area, as I do. Rephrasing helped me quite a bit: "God as I *don't* understand Him" and "turn my will and my life over to the care of *Good.*"

These two ideas let a heathen like me dismiss the religious question and begin to experience the spiritual benefits of A.A. For many of

us, our understanding of God ends at the frustrating point of *not* understanding Him. It was a great relief to me to learn that I simply didn't
have to understand. After all, you don't have to know how a tree grows
to make a fence out of wood. And A.A. *is* practical. Trying to understand God before putting Step Three to work is my idea of an impossible
task. And impractical.

Practically, then, how can one work this Step? My suggestion is
that it's helpful to *stop trying* to work it. Why? Because trying to work
Step Three may be nothing more than another way of trying to understand God. Again, that's impractical.

Many people are determined to make work out of things that
require no work. We have come to believe that nothing good comes without effort and that self-indulgence is always bad. My opinion is that Step
Three requires no work at all and that it can best be implemented by
the most pleasurable self-indulgence.

Let me illustrate with a little experience that happened to me after
I had been in A.A. for about a year. My job situation was, I thought,
quite bad. I could barely get by on what I made. Suddenly, a new opportunity presented itself. The new job would require a move, and it was
with a company well-known for hiring and firing people without regard
for them. Yet the starting salary would be more than one-third greater
than I was getting. My old job had been a constant and powerful worry
to me from the moment I got sober; at the time of the new offer, I had
been stewing and fretting over it night and day for many months.

I had, in effect, been trying to change the job situation by force
of my own will, writing memos, complaining, attempting to mold the
company to my way of thinking. Well, there were forty people there besides me. I couldn't change them all. Now that offer came and compli-
cated my thinking even more. I didn't want to move; I was becoming
part of a great A.A. group and had found many A.A. friends. I was torn
between the chance for a big salary and the security of an existing job;
between moving to a strange city and remaining with the A.A. friends
I had recently acquired. It may not seem like much of a worry to someone in prison, for instance; but to me, at that time, it was enough to send
me to the doctor's for stomach pills, to ruin my mood, and to totally
disturb my life.

Finally, I went to see a friend in A.A. who had many years of
top-quality sobriety. He didn't talk to me about Step Three—at least, not
by name. What he said was "Why don't you just do nothing for a year?"
I asked him what he meant. He advised me to stay at my present job. He
suggested that I simply stop worrying about whether I was making
enough money or not, that I just go to work every day, enjoy the luxury

of not worrying about my situation, take each day as it came, and do what seemed best that day under the circumstances—and do this for one year. Think of that! A year off from worrying! Better than a paid vacation.

Well, I did it. I was so tired of worrying about that lousy job that it was a pleasure just to go to work each day and not worry. In other words, I gave up—but in a very healthful way. My mood improved and so did my work. By the end of the year, I had been promoted twice and had twice been given a salary increase. I have since moved to another company, but with good feelings between me and my former associates.

That was the most valuable year of my life. I learned in the most practical way the truth of that old cliché that you can change only yourself, not the rest of the world. I learned that you can work Step Three by not trying to work it. You can work it by taking a year off from worrying. At the end of the year, if you've enjoyed not-worrying enough, take another year off. Each of us has to do something each day—work in an office or a factory, soldier, take care of a house, or whatever. None of us has to understand God or worry about things beyond our control. We can indulge ourselves in the luxury of not-worrying. Any of us can handle just one day; all each of us has to try at is our own job, our own family life. We don't have to try fixing up the whole world or understanding what no theologian of any faith has ever understood.

We simply stop messing in God's business. And in my opinion, when we stop messing and stop worrying, we *have* turned our will and our lives over to God (or Good) as we understand (or don't understand) Him.

San Jose, California

ECSTASY

We ought not to settle for tepid A.A., for half-measures in taking the Steps, or for too much of the stale and flat in our sober days. Not if we want to stay sober.

No, I think we have to keep looking for something better than dullness, better than average living, better than mediocre spirituality. In an article called "The Search for Ecstasy," written for the A.A. Grapevine, philosopher Gerald Heard said, "It would seem . . . that none of us is living in a sufficiently tonic way, so as to be able to meet the stresses to which we are now bound to be exposed, without breakdown. . . . Alcoholism (like all addictions) is not at base a search for utter sedation. It is a desire for that *ecstasis*, that 'standing out' from the landlocked lagoons of conformity, out onto the uncharted high seas where the only map is the star-set heavens."

Breathes there anywhere a sober alcoholic for whom this passage is not deeply meaningful?

A few years ago, I sat in a New York bar talking to a newspaperman who had just lost another job for drinking. He was interested in my A.A. story. But he was lit up like a Christmas tree, angry, and thoroughly uninterested in any gab about regenerating *him*—that day.

A thought came to me. I said, "You know, H——, I think one of the great pleasures of way-out drinking is just that feeling of being miles apart from the boobs. You're running on a different track. Different clock. Different music. Really existentialist kick. On the knife's edge of pleasure-pain, progress-disaster." And more stuff to that effect.

I saw that I had an attentive listener at last. H. said that that was it exactly. It was living way-out that appealed to him, disasters or no. Living like the boobs was a bore, a drag, an accursed impossibility.

I think now that this thoroughly unsuccessful Twelfth Step effort (I pray H. may be in A.A. somewhere by now) helped *me*. I've never since stopped being aware of the fact that as an alcoholic I had better not set my sights on being just like everybody else, just as ordinary, just as unleavened. As a matter of fact, I don't really know anything about being ordinary—that is, nonalcoholic—so I ought not to set up some phony idea in my mind about normal living. No, let me stick with Mr. Heard's approach for a while. His emphasis is the one for me.

If as an alcoholic I am to "stand out from the landlocked lagoons of conformity" and stay sober, how am I to do it? Join a revolutionary gang? Go hippie? Take up Yoga?

Ah, but I *have* an answer. Take the Twelve Steps. Dull? Have I tried it? I certainly didn't attempt much beyond the first three Steps my first couple of years in A.A. My reaction to the last nine Steps was that they were put in to round out the picture; they were pious rather than practical. One hardly needed to go *that* far . . . and so on.

But I had, along the way, a bit of perverse luck. I got into some rather heavy weather: Job, health, family, everything seemed to go soberly haywire all at once. And I was moved (I see it now as a spiritual shove) to try the Fourth and Fifth Steps, inventory and confession. I didn't do a good job. I wrote some of the inventory, but not all of it. I told some of the wrongs, the pressing ones—but not all. Nonetheless, I had an exciting year of spiritual progress out of it. I was in some important way *changed*.

There came a slowdown, as evidently there always must. I began to think Steps Six and Seven needed more work. Interesting. Difficult.

Existentialist. Knife-edge of disaster-progress. Strange new awareness of God, of self.

I saw that there could be no "lagoons of conformity" for the man who will face his character, confess it, become willing to change it, and ask God to change it.

Dynamite! Dare I set it off? Can't I just sort of let the whole thing go, and settle for modest, quiet, unexceptionable, not very spiritual, average living? After all, X can and Y can and Z can.

Are they alcoholics? Well, no. And do I really know anything about their spiritual lives? Well, no.

Back to me. I needed to be *other*. That's why I drank. I still need to be other. Having tried the toxic way of drugs and excess, let me try the "tonic" (in Heard's phrasing) way of the Steps, the way of health and joy. The Steps are the specific medicine for the thing that's wrong (or right—it doesn't matter) with me: alcoholism. They are the way to be other—and sane into the bargain.

I've come this far: I know now that what is involved in taking the A.A. program entire, as the early A.A.'s gave it to us, is not the prospect of turning into some sort of repulsive goody-goody. It's the threat of being truly alive, aware, and even perhaps *ecstatic*. I'm coming to believe that if I do not accept all of what this program offers (demands?), but instead walk away from it as somehow more than I bargained for, I might get drunk.

In other words, if I do not take A.A.'s Twelve Steps seriously and in full, I cannot expect to be "on the program."

Vermont

"NO MAN IS AN ISLAND"

I was spiritually bankrupt long before A.A. entered my life and long before alcoholism took over like a parasite under my skin. I had nothing, no faith at all to cling to. I had no faith in man, because along with my drinking I had lost faith in myself. I trusted no one, for others were but a mere reflection of my own self, and I could not trust *me*.

I got sober in A.A., and, like a miracle, the warm flood of reality I had feared for so long flowed over me, and I was no longer afraid. I began to wonder why. Along with sobriety, something new had come into my life.

I began to have *concern* for others. This word "concern," along with its sister *consideration*, was an alien thing to me. I had believed myself capable of falling in love; I had thought myself a loving mother; but these emotions, I now perceive, had been reflections of my own self-interest. Nothing penetrated beyond my self. I began, in early sobriety, to feel *compassion* for other drunks, then for my children, then for my ex-husband. This compassion, a feeling accompanied later by love, opened up the door to a huge fortress within me which had been forever locked.

Now this was the strange thing: I was not, in sobriety, returning to my former state. I was not resuming a "well" state which I had left when I began to drink alcoholically. I was becoming, as I heard it put once, "weller than well." In probing (via the Fourth Step) into my own personality, I found a new substance inside me. It had never been there before, even in childhood. Either a stone or an empty hole had been where it should have grown.

Now something was taking root. I began to *feel* for others, to be able, for very brief moments, to put myself in their shoes. New worlds opened up. I began to understand the world about me. I was not the center of the universe. (What a calamity it seemed to discover that!) I was part of a gigantic, wonderful mystery. I could not probe it, because I knew nothing about it. I could only circle it with a childlike curiosity. I am still circling about it. I shall never, nor shall any of us, discover the secrets of the universe. But we can *accept* their mystery, our part in them, and our lives and deaths, as something spiritual beyond our understanding.

I began to watch my children. They were small, important people. I realized I had never treated them while I was drinking as anything more than little machines I had created, as if I had erected part of a Meccano set and been proud of it. I saw them begin to blossom as my treatment of them changed. I reached out a hand to help someone, sometimes even only by listening, and I felt a strange contentment at being able to help —an incredible discovery for me!

I learned my own version of what spirituality is. It does not mean I have to be like the saints who claimed to have direct advice and visions from God. It means I have to be concerned with my fellowman; through this alone can I receive the grace of God, my Higher Power, for, in the words of John Donne, so long before A.A., "No man is an island."

I began to feel a safety in my new spiritual feelings, until I was shaken up one night by an A.A. friend who said, "All right, so you can apply the Third Step and a spiritual belief in God to your personal life, but how can you accept the terrible calamities which happen around us every day?"

I was faced again, perilously, with the questions of my religious but nonspiritual childhood—how can I accept a belief in a God who allows such monstrous crimes against man as the black scenes at Buchenwald, Dachau, Hiroshima? I began to think frighteningly of death and suffering, not my own, but all humanity's. I began to question my new beliefs too much—I began to panic. I began to read beyond A.A.'s literature for answers.

Fortunately for me, before I had read too much about the subject of spiritual beliefs (an area which was only leading me to confusion), I realized I was asking for too much too soon. Wisely, I left the philosophy books to minds more capable than mine. I could not risk further mental confusion. I returned to the teachings of A.A., which had already saved me from a life of torment.

I needed to look no further than the Twelve Steps and the powerful wording of our Serenity Prayer, "to accept the things we cannot change." My personal answer is there in the word "accept." Accept man's place in the universal scheme. Accept my life as one minute particle of the whole. None of us can ever fathom the glories and the uncharted regions of the universe. But we *can* live on earth and love one another. We can let in the beginnings of *concern, compassion, consideration,* and watch ourselves grow. With the tools and guideposts of Alcoholics Anonymous, we can learn a little of this precious gift—our gateway to human spirituality.

New York, New York

The
Twelve
Steps

1. We admitted we were powerless over alcohol . . . that our lives had become unmanageable.

2. Came to believe that a Power greater than ourselves could restore us to sanity.

3. Made a decision to turn our will and our lives over to the care of God *as we understood Him.*

4. Made a searching and fearless moral inventory of ourselves.

5. Admitted to God, to ourselves, and to another human being the exact nature of our wrongs.

6. Were entirely ready to have God remove all these defects of character.

7. Humbly asked Him to remove our shortcomings.

8. Made a list of all persons we had harmed and became willing to make amends to them all.

9. Made direct amends to such people wherever possible, except when to do so would injure them or others.

10. Continued to take personal inventory and when we were wrong promptly admitted it.

11. Sought through prayer and meditation to improve our conscious contact with God *as we understood Him,* praying only for knowledge of His will for us and the power to carry that out.

12. Having had a spiritual awakening as the result of these Steps, we tried to carry this message to alcoholics, and to practice these principles in all our affairs.